GW00391606

PRESENTED TO

Robyn

BY

A

ON THE OCCASION OF

ON THIS DAY

PROMISES FOR KIDS FROM
THE BOOK
WITH THE 'VERBS

Richard L. Osborne

 Tyndale House Publishers, Inc.
Wheaton, Illinois

Scripture quotations from *The Living Bible,*
copyright 1971 held by assignment to Illinois
Regional Bank N.A. (as trustee). All rights
reserved. Bible promises compiled and arranged
by Richard Osborne. Illustrations by Chris
Kielesinski and Terry VanRoon. 'Verbs copyright
1985 by Impartation Idea, Inc.

First printing, October 1988
Library of Congress Catalog Card Number 88-51083
ISBN 0-8423-5053-5
Copyright 1988 by Tyndale House Publishers, Inc.
Printed in the United States of America

CONTENTS

INTRODUCING THE 'VERBS

The 'Verbs were created to illustrate scriptural principles in a humorous and easy-to-learn way. Each character represents an element or attitude found in God's Word.

MR. WISDOM
He represents God's wisdom and is ready to teach all who will hear him.

BIG and BIGGER
They represent the rewards of staying on God's path and the results of wandering off it. They often do silly things to get the point across.

SPORT, SMILEY, JOY and BABY 'VERB
These characters represent those who want God's best and are following his path for their lives.

B.A. (BAD ATTITUDE)
He represents those who reject wisdom. He's unteachable and always does things his own way.

A MESSAGE
FOR PARENTS

This book was written to bring joy to your task of teaching your children about God's promises.

Some have said that the Bible contains 3,000 promises; others have said over 30,000! What is a Bible promise? This is difficult to pin down, for God always varies his presentation. In this book, 200 important promises and principles have been put together so that your children can get started on the long and wonderful road to realizing God's faithfulness.

This book has two parts. The second part, "Promises from the Book," is the largest. Each page has a full-color 'Verbs illustration to accompany the teaching from the Bible. In addition, the "Footprints" at the bottom of each page will help your child "make tracks" through the Bible. They contain practical comments and other good Bible references. Story numbers refer to stories in *The Book for Children* by Kenneth N. Taylor. Use the Footprints to help explain, illustrate, and further develop the meaning and reality of the promise. Each topical section of promises ends with a "Making Tracks" page. These pages contain songs, poems, games, and famous quotes from the Bible. Use these pages to sum up the teaching of that section, reinforcing for your child the truths from God's Word.

The first part of this book, "Receiving God's Promises," is perhaps the most important. This section contains six stories from the Bible that illustrate how God's promises work out in people's lives. Each story is accompanied by a lesson that will help your child better understand God's promises and how to receive them. If you read these stories and explain their lessons to your children over and over again, they'll never have to go without anything that God has promised.

This book can be used in devotional times with your children. Older children will be able to read the words for them-

9

selves, and kids of all ages will enjoy the pictures! Also, when a child is in need of God's help in a particular area, go to the index and find the promise that covers the child's need. Then pray with your child and watch the results!

As a parent, you hold the hand of your child until you transfer that grasp to God's mighty hand. This book is a tool that will help you do that effectively.

RECEIVING GOD'S PROMISES

JESUS ON THE EMMAUS ROAD

Late in the afternoon, three days after Jesus had been crucified, two of Jesus' friends were walking to the village of Emmaus. It was about seven miles from Jerusalem. They were talking to each other about all the strange things that had happened that day. Then Jesus came and walked along with them. But he looked different, so they didn't recognize him. "What are you talking about that makes you so sad?" he asked them. One of them, named Cleopas, answered, "Are you a stranger here, that you haven't heard all the things that have been happening the last few days?"

"What things?" Jesus asked.

"About Jesus of Nazareth," they replied. "He was a prophet and did great miracles. We thought he was the one who would free Israel from the Romans. But the chief priests and other Jewish leaders crucified him. And now, early this morning, three days after he was killed, some women who are friends of ours went to the cave where he was buried and came back reporting that his body wasn't there. And they said that some angels told them he is alive! Some of our men went to the tomb afterward and found it was as the women had said; Jesus' body wasn't there!"

Then Jesus said to them, "You are such foolish, foolish people! You find it so hard to believe all that the prophets wrote in the Scriptures! Wasn't it clearly predicted by the prophets that the Messiah would have to suffer all these things before entering his time of glory?"

Then Jesus quoted them passage after passage from the writings of the prophets, beginning with the book of Genesis and going right on through the Scriptures. He explained what the passages meant and what they said about himself. But still his two friends didn't recognize him.

As they neared the village where the men lived, Jesus prepared to leave them and go on further. Thinking he was a traveler they invited him to spend the night with them, as it was getting late in the day. So he went home with them. As they were eating supper together, Jesus took a small loaf of bread, and after he thanked God for it, he broke it and gave it to them. But as he did this, suddenly they recognized him and then he disappeared!

They started back to Jerusalem and right away found Jesus' disciples and others with them, and they told them how they had seen Jesus and talked with him and how they had recognized him as he was breaking the bread at the supper table. And just then, while they were telling about it, Jesus himself suddenly appeared among them and spoke to them!

They were badly frightened, for they thought he was a ghost. Then he said to them, "Look at the nail marks in my hands and my feet. Touch me and see that it is I, myself, for a ghost doesn't have flesh and bones as you see I have!" Still they stood there undecided, filled with joy and doubt. Then he asked them, "Do you have anything here to eat?" They gave him a piece of broiled fish, and he ate it as they watched! Then he said, "When I was with you before, don't you remember my telling you that everything written about me by Moses and the prophets and in the Psalms must all come true?" Then he opened their minds to understand at last these many Scriptures! And he said, "Yes, it was written long ago that the Messiah must suffer and die and rise again from the dead on the third day; and that this message of salvation should be taken from Jerusalem to all the nations: There is forgiveness of sins for all who turn to me. You have seen these prophecies come true."

Mark 16 Luke 24 Story 178

God's Word Is True   While Jesus was here on earth he spoke about the Scriptures and quoted them as God's inspired words. He said that they would all come true. And in the story you just read he called two of his followers foolish for not believing the Scriptures.

The apostle Paul wrote this about the Scriptures, "The whole Bible was given to us by inspiration from God and is useful to teach us what is true and to make us realize what is wrong in our lives; it straightens us out and helps us do what is right. It is God's way of making us well prepared at every point, fully equipped to do good to everyone."

And Peter wrote, "No prophecy recorded in Scripture was ever thought up by the prophet himself. It was the Holy Spirit

The Disappearing

within these godly men who gave them true messages from God."

The Bible which you read from today is the inspired Word of God. It was written over a period of 1,500 years and is a collection of sixty-six different books written by approximately forty different men. Only God could plan a book like that and still have every part fit perfectly together and agree with all the other parts.

So follow Jesus' example by believing everything that God's Word says and promises. Then God will open your mind to understand the Scriptures just as Jesus did for his disciples, and you will become wise, too.

Luke 24 2 Timothy 3:16 2 Peter 1:21

ABRAHAM'S GREAT TEST

One day God told Abram, "I am your friend." So Abram reminded his great friend that he wanted a son for he had no children. God promised to give him one.

Then he took Abram out under the night skies. He told him to look up at the stars and asked him whether he could count them. Abram couldn't do it because there were so many. Then God told him, "You will not only have one son; you will have many, many grandchildren and great-grandchildren. Their families will be like those stars up there—too many to count!"

Abraham (whose name God had changed from "Abram") was one hundred years old when his son Isaac was born. What a happy day it was! God had kept his promise.

One day, many years later, God said to Abraham, "Abraham, take your son Isaac whom you love so much, and go to the land of Moriah and burn him as a sacrifice upon one of the mountains I will point out to you!"

How could Abraham ever do this? How could he kill his own dear son? But God had told him to do it; Abraham heard him speak. He knew that he must do whatever God said.

So Abraham got up early in the morning and saddled his donkey. He took two young men with him, some wood to lay on the altar, and Isaac his son.

They started towards the mountain God had told him about. They traveled all that day and the next before Abraham finally saw the mountain far ahead of them. Then he told the young men to stop and wait. He and Isaac would go to the mountain and worship, he told them, and then they would come back to them.

Why do you think Abraham said that both of them would come back? Because he still trusted in God and his promises. He was ready to kill his son Isaac, through whom God had promised to give him a whole nation of descendants. For he believed that if Isaac died, God would bring him back to life again, in order to keep his promise.

Isaac did not know what God had told his father to do, nor

why his father was taking him to the mountain. He knew they were going to offer a burnt offering, but he didn't know he was going to be burned up on the altar as a sacrifice. So, as they walked along together, he said to his father, "Father, we have the fire and the wood, but where is the lamb for a burnt offering?"

Abraham answered, "My son, God will find himself a lamb for the burnt offering."

When they came to the place God had sent them to, Abraham built an altar and laid wood on it. Then he tied Isaac and laid him on the wood, and Abraham lifted the knife to kill his son. . . .

But at that instant the angel of God shouted to him from heaven. "Abraham! Abraham! Stop!" Then the angel told him not to hurt Isaac. Abraham had proved that he trusted God and believed that God would always keep his promises.
Genesis 21–22 Hebrews 11:17-19 Stories 7, 9, 10

God Always Keeps His Promises   In this story Abraham was so certain that God would always keep his promises that he was willing to kill his only son, Isaac, because he trusted God even when he didn't understand what God was doing. He knew that not even death could get in the way of God keeping his promise.

Sometimes when it looks as if God's promise is not coming true, you might start thinking, "Oh well, God does whatever he wants to, and I guess for some reason he doesn't want to fulfill his promise to me." While it's true that God does whatever he wants to, once he decides what he's going to do and promises to do it, you can be sure he will stay true to his word. So when you ask him to do something he has already promised to do, he doesn't think about whether he wants to do it or not, he just does it for you. The writer of Hebrews put it this way: "God bound himself with an oath, so that those he promised to help would be perfectly sure and never need to wonder whether he might change his plans."

He has given us both his promise and his oath, two things we can completely count on, for it is impossible for God to tell a lie.

So search the Bible and find all that God has promised to

do for you. You can know without a doubt that he will do all that he has promised. He won't miss even the smallest detail of the smallest promise, for if he said it, his Spirit will make it all come true.

Isaiah 34:16 Hebrews 6:17-18

THE MIRACLE VICTORY

The armies of the kings of Moab, Ammon, and Mount Seir declared war on King Jehoshaphat and the people of Judah. When word reached Jehoshaphat that a vast army was marching against him, he was badly shaken by the news. He determined to ask the Lord for help; so he announced that all the people of Judah should go without food for a time and come to Jerusalem to pray with him. People from all across the nation came, and as they gathered at the new court of the Temple, Jehoshaphat stood among them and prayed this prayer:

"O Lord God of our fathers—the only God in all the heavens, the Ruler of all the kingdoms of the earth—you are so powerful, so mighty. Who can stand against you? O our God, didn't you drive out the heathen who lived in this land when your people arrived? And didn't you give this land forever to the descendants of your friend Abraham? Your people settled here and built this temple for you. They believed that whenever we are faced with any calamity, such as war, disease, or famine, we can stand before you here at this temple and cry out to you to save us, and that you will hear us and rescue us.

"And now see what the armies of Moab, Ammon, and Mount Seir are doing. They have come to throw us out of your land which you have given us. We have no way to protect ourselves against this mighty army. We don't know what to do, but we are looking to you."

As the people from every part of Judah stood before the Lord with their wives and children, the Spirit of the Lord came upon the prophet Jahaziel. "Listen to me, all you people of Judah and Jerusalem and you, O king Jehoshaphat!" he explained. "The Lord says, 'Don't be afraid! Don't be paralyzed by this mighty army! For the battle is not yours, but God's! Tomorrow, go down and attack them! But you will not need to fight. Take your places; stand quietly and see the incredible rescue operation God will perform for you! Don't be afraid or discouraged! Go out there tomorrow, for the Lord is with you!' "

Then King Jehoshaphat and all the people worshiped the Lord with songs of praise that rang out strong and clear.

Early the next morning king Jehoshaphat called everyone to attention. "Listen to me," he said. "Believe in the Lord your God, and you will have success! Believe his prophets, and everything will be all right!"

With the choir leading the march, singing "His Loving Kindness Is Forever," they walked along praising and thanking the Lord! And at the moment they began to sing and to praise, the Lord caused the armies of Ammon, Moab, and Mount Seir to begin fighting among themselves, and they destroyed each other! So when the army of Judah arrived at the watchtower that looks out over the wilderness, as far as they could look there were dead bodies lying on the ground— not a single one of the enemy had escaped.
2 Chronicles 20

Praying for God's Promises King Jehoshaphat knew how to pray for God's promises! If we look carefully, we will be able to see a "recipe" with seven important steps. First, he decided to *trust* God to solve his problem. Second, he *reminded* God of his promise: God had given the land forever to the descendants of Abraham, and he would rescue them if they came before him at the Temple and asked for his help. Jehoshaphat confidently said, "You will hear us and rescue us!" He *believed* that God would keep his promise. Third, he *told* God the problem and asked him for a solution. Fourth, he *waited* to see if God had any instructions. Fifth, he *thanked* and *praised* God for the answer before it actually happened. Sixth, he showed that he believed God by *following* his instructions and *acting* like God had truly answered his prayer. If he hadn't really believed, he wouldn't have taken his small army out to meet such a huge enemy army. The last thing he did was *watch* God keep his promise.

Once you find yourself in need of something God has promised, follow Jehoshaphat's recipe for success.
1. Decide that you are going to trust God for the solution.
2. Find the promises of God that apply to your need and remind God of them believing that he will keep his promise.
3. Tell God what you need.

4. Be quiet and wait to see if God has any instructions. There is usually a feeling of peace when you have faith that God has heard and answered you.
5. Thank God that he has heard your prayer and taken care of your need.
6. Act like God has answered you. Don't be afraid or discouraged; wait patiently for God's help.
7. Watch God keep his promise.

Through all this, remember the last thing Jehoshaphat said to his people before seeing God's solution: "Believe in the Lord your God, and you will have success! Believe his prophets, and everything will be all right!"

DAVID'S LONG WAIT

The Lord told Samuel that he would not let Saul continue as king because he had disobeyed the Lord. He told him to go to Bethlehem and anoint one of Jesse's sons as the new king. Samuel obeyed the Lord and went to Jesse's house to meet his sons.

When they came, Samuel thought that Jesse's oldest son was the one the Lord would choose because he was such a fine-looking young man. But the Lord told him no, he was not the one. Then Jesse presented in order of age his next six sons. But Samuel said, "The Lord has not chosen any of these. Are these all the sons you have?"

"No," Jesse answered, "there is one other, the youngest, but he is out taking care of the sheep."

"Send for him," Samuel said. So they brought in David. Then the Lord said to Samuel, "Anoint him, for this is the one."

Not too long after, David killed the giant Philistine, Goliath, and Saul made him a leader in his army. I'm sure this looked to David like the beginning of his promotion to king. But one day as David and King Saul were traveling together, some women came out and sang songs about their victories. They said that King Saul had killed thousands of their enemies but David had killed ten thousands! Saul was very angry about this, and from then on he was jealous of David. He made David stay away from him and wouldn't let David fight in the army. Saul even tried to kill David twice by throwing his spear at him. Despite this, David succeeded in everything he did because the Lord was with him.

When Saul tried several more times to kill him, David had to escape through a window and run for his life.

Saul and his men chased David for years trying to kill him. David became a fugitive living in the wilderness. Once Saul took three thousand of his soldiers to hunt for David. He ended up going into the same cave where David and his men were hiding! Saul didn't know they were there, of course, so he walked into the cave alone to sleep. David's men wanted to kill Saul, but David said, "Don't kill him, for who can attack the Lord's chosen king? He will die some day in battle or of old age, but God forbid that I should kill God's chosen king." So David snuck up behind Saul and cut off a piece of Saul's robe, then hid again.

When Saul woke up and left the cave, David shouted to him and held up the piece of robe. When Saul saw that David could have killed him but that he was kind and spared his life instead, Saul stopped trying to kill him.

Soon afterwards, Saul's hatred for David returned, and he tried even harder to kill David. David had to pretend he was a traitor and go and live with the Philistines to get away from Saul. While all this was happening David knew in his heart that he was supposed to be the king.

Then, when Saul was killed in a war with the Philistines, David became the king of Judah. But it was another seven years before he became the king of all Israel; the position God had anointed him for many years earlier.

1 Samuel 16–20 2 Samuel 5 Stories 80–89

Faith and Patience If it wasn't for faith and patience, David would have given up, and he would never have become the king of Israel. His faith kept God's plan for his life real in his heart and mind. And patience gave him the strength to go through everything that came his way while he waited for God to make that plan real.

Faith is being completely sure that something you are hoping for is going to happen.

If someone who never broke their promises, promised to take you out to the park on the weekend, the weekend would come and you would be all ready to go. That's faith. Having faith in God is simply realizing that he will always do whatever he has promised to do.

And patience is the ability to hold your head up and keep your faith strong no matter what happens or how long it takes.

You will develop strength of character and trust God more each time you use it. Patience will make your faith strong and steady. The two together are powerful. The writer of Hebrews said, "Follow the example of those who receive all that God has promised them because of their strong faith and patience."

JERUSALEM
Tour Map

That's what David did. He believed what God had promised him and then patiently waited for him to make it real.
Romans 5:3-5 Hebrews 6:12, 15 / 11:1

JOSEPH IN PRISON AND PALACE

One of Jacob's twelve sons was named Joseph. Joseph was his father's favorite son, so Jacob gave him a beautiful coat as a present. This made his brothers very jealous.

One night Joseph had a strange dream. He dreamed that the sun, the moon, and eleven stars all bowed to him. When he told his brothers about it they thought Joseph was saying that the eleven of them should bow to him as though he were their king. They became very angry.

One day, Joseph's father sent him to Shechem to see how his brothers were doing with the sheep. When his brothers saw him coming, they began talking to each other about killing him. Just then, they saw some men coming who were taking things to Egypt to sell. The brothers said, "Let's sell Joseph to them! We'll get rid of him and get some money, too."

So they got twenty pieces of silver, and the merchants put Joseph on a camel and took him far away to the land of Egypt.

The brothers dipped Joseph's beautiful coat in some animal's blood and told their father that a wild animal must have eaten him. Joseph's father cried.

When Joseph arrived in Egypt, he was sold as a slave to a man named Potiphar. The Lord helped Joseph work hard. His master was pleased with him and put him in charge of all his other servants. But when Potiphar's wife told a lie about Joseph, Potiphar put him in jail. Yet the Lord was with him there too. The jailer soon handed over the entire prison to him, so that all the other prisoners were responsible to Joseph.

While two of Pharaoh's officers were in jail because Pharaoh was mad at them, they both had strange dreams. God gave Joseph the ability to tell them exactly what their dreams meant.

Two years later when king Pharaoh had a strange dream, one of the officers remembered Joseph and told the king about him. Pharaoh had Joseph brought to him right away.

Joseph told him that his dream meant there would be seven good years of wonderful crops, when everyone's gardens would grow. But after that there would be seven bad years when nothing would grow.

He told Pharaoh to put someone in charge of saving up corn in Egypt during the seven good years. Then during the hungry years, the people would have enough food. The king thought this was a good idea, and he put Joseph in charge. In fact, Pharaoh put him in charge of all the land of Egypt, and made Joseph almost as important as himself.

For seven years, Joseph made all the farmers give corn to Pharaoh, and he stored it in big cities. When the seven bad years came, he sold it to the people as they needed it.

Far away, Joseph's family ran out of food, and his father sent Joseph's brothers to Egypt to buy some. Since Joseph was the governor of Egypt, he was in charge of selling food to the people. His brothers didn't recognize him in his Egyptian robes, but Joseph knew them right away. He pretended he didn't know them at all. Then he said, "You are spies and have come here to see what trouble we are in, so that you can bring an army and attack us." He put them in jail for three days. On the third day Joseph called his brothers before him. He told them all but one of them could return home to their father. The brother in prison would be released only if their youngest brother Benjamin returned with them to Egypt the next time they needed food.

After many hard days of travel, Joseph's brothers finally returned home and told their father what had happened. Their father said Benjamin, the youngest, couldn't go. For since he thought Joseph was dead, he said that he couldn't bear it if anything happened to Benjamin.

But when they ran out of food again Jacob had to agree. So Benjamin went with his brothers back to Egypt. While they were there, Joseph made it look like Benjamin had stolen something from him. He said that the rest could go home but Benjamin must stay in Egypt as his slave.

Joseph did this to see if his brothers had changed since they sold him as a slave. They all bowed down and begged Joseph to let Benjamin go and make them slaves instead. They didn't want to break their father's heart. They had shown

Joseph that they had changed. When they bowed down Joseph remembered his dream. God had brought Joseph right where he was supposed to be. He was using him to save his whole family from starvation.

Then Joseph told his brothers who he really was. What excitement! They all kissed and hugged each other. Joseph sent them home to get their father and their families, and they all came and lived in the richest part of Egypt with all the food they needed.
Genesis 37–47 Stories 19–25

God's Growth Plan   When God first began to show Joseph the plan for his life in a dream, Joseph still had a lot of growing to do before it could happen.

After he was sold by his brothers he was made a slave in a rich man's house. He worked hard, learned, and grew until he was in charge of the whole house and all the other slaves.

Then he was given a bigger challenge. After being put in prison he continued to work hard and learn, until he was in charge of the whole prison and all the prisoners. Not only was he in charge, but everyone liked him as well. And in prison he had the chance to interpret some other dreams before he was brought to Pharaoh. God took Joseph through a growth plan so that when he stood in front of Pharaoh he knew how to hear the meaning of Pharaoh's dream from God. He had God's wisdom to know what to do and the experience to be in charge of the whole project.

Whenever you trust God for something he has promised you, big or small, he begins to fit it into his growth plan for your life. For he won't give you anything that you are not ready for. So concentrate on growing and learning and God will bring his promises into your life at the perfect time. Remember what the Apostle Paul said, "We know that all that happens to us is working for our good if we love God and are fitting into his plans."
Romans 8:28

Isaac, the Miracle Baby

God spoke to Abram in a vision and this is what he told him: "Don't be fearful, Abram, for I will defend you. And I will give you great blessings."

But Abram replied, "O Lord, what good are all your blessings when I have no son to share them with?" Then God told him, "You will have a son. Look up into the heavens and count the stars if you can. Your children and their children and all their descendants will be like that—too many to count!" Abram believed God, and God considered him perfect in his sight because of his faith in God.

But Sarai and Abram had no children. So Sarai took her maid, an Egyptian girl named Hagar, and gave her to Abram to be his second wife.

"Since the Lord has given me no children," Sarai said, "have Hagar as your wife as well, and any children she has will be mine."

So Hagar had a son, and Abram named him Ishmael.

Thirteen years later when Abram was ninety-nine years old, God appeared to him and told him, "I am changing your name. It is no longer 'Abram' (which means 'Exalted Father') but 'Abraham' (which means 'Father of Nations') for that is what you will be. And regarding Sarai your wife—her name is no longer 'Sarai' but 'Sarah' (which means 'Princess'). I will bless her and give you a son from her, she will be the mother of nations!"

Abraham thanked the Lord, but inside he was laughing. "Me be a father?" he said in amusement. "Me a hundred years old? And Sarah, to have a baby at ninety?"

And Abraham said to God, "Please, bless Ishmael!" "No," God replied, "that isn't what I said. Sarah will have a son; and you are to name him Isaac (which means 'Laughter'). My promises to you are for him and his descendants. As for Ishmael, I will bless him also, just as you have asked me to. But my contract is with Isaac, who will be born to you and Sarah next year at about this time."

Then God did as he had promised, and Sarah became pregnant and gave Abraham a baby son in his old age, at the time God had said. And Abraham named him Isaac.

And Sarah declared, "God has brought me laughter! All who hear about this will be happy with me. For who would have dreamed that I would ever have a baby? Yet I have given Abraham a child in his old age!"
Genesis 15–17, 21

God's Promises Are for You Today

Do you remember some of the parables that Jesus told? They were stories with meanings that Jesus used to teach the people who gathered to hear him. Some of the stories in the Old Testament have meanings like that too. God didn't make the stories up, but he did cause things to happen in people's lives that have meaning for us today. Can you see how God was teaching you about Jesus with the things that happened in Joseph's life? Now in this last story you can learn who God's promises were meant for. Abraham had two children: Ishmael, who was born because Abraham wanted a son of his own, and then Isaac, who was born because of God's promise that he would give Abraham a son.

The birth of Ishmael is like people who try to live on their own without God's help. But the birth of Isaac represents those who trust in God's promises. In the story, God promises to bless Isaac because he was born by God's promise. And what God is saying is that he will bless us, too, when we trust in his promises. He invites us to become a part of his family, the church.

The apostle Paul said, "Everyone is invited to belong to God's church, and all of God's promises of mighty blessings through Christ apply to everyone who accepts the Good News about Christ and what he has done for them."
Galatians 3:16-18 / 4:22-28 Ephesians 3:6-7

PROMISES FROM THE BOOK

PART ONE

SLEEP

GOD GIVES US SLEEP

Night is the time God gave for you to sleep. It is not healthy to stay up late and get up too early. God wants you to get your proper rest. *1 Thessalonians 5:7 Psalm 127:2*

Footprint   Even with all the things Jesus needed to do, he still got his proper sleep. *Mark 5:35-41*

38

PEACEFUL SLEEP

You can lie down in peace and go to sleep. For the Lord is with you and watching over you. You are safe, for God himself is caring for you. *Psalms 3:5 / 4:8 / 121:3-4*

Footprint Remember Jacob's dream? God was with him even while he was sleeping. *Genesis 28:10-33 Story 15*

GOD WILL GUARD YOU WHILE YOU SLEEP

All night long God protects you, and the good things you have learned will guard you and keep you safe. With these things guarding your thoughts, you can sleep without fear.
Proverbs 3:24-26 / 6:22-24

Footprint When you know God's promises, there is nothing to be afraid of, and if you are not afraid, your dreams will be sweet.

40

GOD IS NOT CHANGED BY THE DARK

God is your shield; his promises are your armor. You don't need to be afraid of the dark anymore. Danger and evil will not touch you for God is watching over you. *Psalm 91*

Footprint   Remember the night Daniel spent in the lions' den? Even with hungry lions all around him, I'm sure he slept well because he trusted God. *Daniel 6 Story 135*

SLEEPING SOON

VERSE 1

♩ = 92

Lord, _____ I'm ly - ing still, Look-ing at moon-light in my dark - ened room. Thanks for be - ing _ here, I'll be sleep - ing soon.

CHORUS

You give me peace - ful _ sleep, I'm safe with you in the dark. _____ Your dreams guide _ me, I know that I'll be dream-ing soon.

Repeat Verse 1 at end

VERSE 2
You are watching over me,
My eyes are tired of looking 'round my room.
You will never sleep,
I'll be dreaming soon.

VERSE 3
Lord, you talk to me,
You give me dreams in my darkened room.
They are guiding me,
I'll be sleeping soon.

PART TWO
YOU AND GOD

GOD WILL NEVER LEAVE YOU

God will never fail you or leave you. He is the one who created you; you are his. When you go through troubles and problems, he will be with you and will help you come through them. For he is your God, and you are precious to him.
Hebrews 13:5 Isaiah 43:1-5

Footprint   Remember Joshua? One of the first things God said to him when he became Israel's leader was "I will be with you." *Joshua 1:1-9 Story 57*

44

GOD IS PATIENT WITH YOU

God is patient with you. He forgives your sins and keeps on loving you no matter what you do. His patience gives you time to learn and to grow. *Numbers 14:17-18 Romans 2:4*

Footprint   God always hopes that people will want to know and love him. He is very patient and loving—even when we make silly mistakes. Read the story about Noah to see just how patient God was with the people while Noah was building the ark. *Genesis 6–8 1 Peter 3:20 Story 4*

GOD DOES NOT GET ANGRY WITH YOU

Though he is sad if you do wrong things, he is always kind and forgiving. *Isaiah 54:9-10 Ezekiel 16:42*

Footprint Even though Peter denied knowing Jesus, Jesus forgave him and gave Peter the chance to say he was sorry. *John 18:15-18, 25-27 Story 174 John 24:1-17*

GOD IS MERCIFUL TO YOU

God forgives all of your sins, heals you, and fills your life with good things. He loves you and treats you tenderly and kindly. And yet you haven't done anything to deserve all of this. That's God's mercy, undeserved kindness.
Psalm 103:1-16 Hebrews 4:16 1 Peter 1:3

Footprint   Saul killed Christians and talked against Jesus. Jesus appeared to him, forgave him, and called him to be a great leader in the church. That's God's mercy! *Acts 8–9 1 Timothy 1:12-15 Story 182*

47

GOD IS KIND TO YOU

Can you imagine a mountain walking away or a hill just disappearing? Well, it would be easier for a mountain to disappear than for God to be unkind to you. God will always be kind to you. *Isaiah 54:10*

Footprint   *Ephesians 2:7* says that God can always point to us as examples of his rich kindness. Think of some of the ways that God has shown you his kindness.

GOD IS YOUR FRIEND

Abraham was called "the friend of God" because he trusted God and obeyed him. Jesus said that when you trust and obey God you become his friend as well.
John 15:13-15 James 2:23

Footprint   Read about God's friendship with Abraham in *Stories 6–10.*

YOU CAN HEAR GOD'S VOICE

A shepherd calls each one of his sheep by name. When they hear him call, they come because they recognize his voice. But if a stranger tries calling the sheep, they will run away.
John 10:3-5, 27

Footprint   In *John 10:3-5* Jesus explains that he is your shepherd and you are his sheep. He'll watch out for you and you will learn to recognize his voice.

50

GOD ALWAYS HAS GOOD THOUGHTS ABOUT YOU

IF I HAD A COOKIE FOR EVERY ONE OF GOD'S THOUGHTS ABOUT ME

It is wonderful to realize that God is thinking about you constantly. You can't even count how many times in a day he thinks about you. And every one of his thoughts and plans for you are good. *Psalms 40:5 / 139:17-18 Jeremiah 29:10-11 2 Peter 5:7*

Footprint   Since God is always thinking about you, you don't need to make an appointment with him. You can talk to God anytime, and he will always hear you. That's prayer.

GOD LOVES YOU

God loves you so much that he sent his only Son to die for you so that you could become his child. And now his love surrounds you like the walls of a fort. His love is strong, and it will never fail. *Psalms 31:21 / 117:2 John 3:16 1 John 3:1*

Footprint God's love for you is so great! Read what God allowed his Son, Jesus, to go through because he loved you and wanted you to become his child. *Matthew 27 Story 176*

52

YOU CAN EXPERIENCE GOD'S LOVE

God wants you to experience his love and discover how long, how wide, how deep, and how high his love for you really is. God's love never ends in any direction. It is so great that before you fully understand it you will be filled up with God himself. *Ephesians 3:18-19 1 John 3:1*

Footprint Will Joy and Smiley ever find all the measurements of God's love? Figure out how deep and wide God's love is in your life.

GOD CARES ABOUT YOU

Don't worry! God himself cares about you. So let him have all your worries and concerns. For he is always thinking about you and watching over every detail of your life.
Psalm 121:5 Matthew 6:30 1 Peter 5:7

Footprint   God is taking care of your problems, so don't worry. Stop and smell the flowers and listen to the birds sing. Then read *Matthew 6:25-34*.

54

GOD IS ALWAYS WITH YOU

God is everywhere, and that means that he is always with you. No matter where you go, God is still there! Whenever you start to feel lonely, remember that God is with you and be happy! *Psalms 16:11 / 139 / 140:13 Acts 3:19*

Footprint   Some people don't like God or are afraid of him because they know they have done bad things. But since Jesus came to wash our sins away, we can enjoy God's presence because he has forgiven our sins. *Hebrews 12:18-24 Exodus 18–20 Story 37*

GOD AND JESUS WILL LIVE WITH YOU

Jesus said, "I will reveal myself to you if you love me and obey me. The Father will love you too, and we will come to you and live with you." *John 14:23*

Footprint   When you become one of God's children, he moves into your life and stays. Moses built a special tent so that God could have a place to meet his people. But now he has packed his bags and moved right in to our hearts!
Exodus 40 2 Corinthians 6:16 Story 42

GOD IS YOUR FATHER

When you became a Christian, God adopted you as his very own child. Now you can call God your heavenly Dad! And if your earthly dad does his best for you, won't your perfect Father in heaven look after you even better?
Luke 11:13 John 1:14 Galatians 4:5-7

Footprint   God has many children now because he was willing to give up his only Son. Does this remind you of another story? *Genesis 22 Story 10*

NOTHING CAN SEPARATE YOU FROM GOD'S LOVE

Nothing can ever separate you from God's love. Death can't, and life can't. The angels won't, and all the powers of hell itself cannot take you away from God's love. You don't need to worry about what might happen tomorrow. Nothing will ever be able to separate you from God's love. *Romans 8:38-39*

Footprint King Nebuchadnezzar tried to separate Shadrach, Meshach, and Abednego from God by ordering them to bow down to him instead to God. You'll love what happened! Read *Daniel 3* and *Story 132*.

58

You Can Get to Know God

Do you want to brag about something? Get to know God, understanding who he is and what he is like—then brag about that! Actually, God is so big that you can spend your whole life getting to know him better and better—and that is what he wants you to do! *Jeremiah 9:24 Philippians 3:7-11*

Footprint   Enoch got to know God so well that one day he just disappeared. God took him to heaven before he died. *Hebrews 11:5-6 Story 3*

GOD KNOWS YOU

God knew you even before you were born. He made you grow in your mother's womb. He knows everything about you—your thoughts, where you are every moment, and even what you are going to say before you say it! *Psalm 139*

Footprint   It is always easy to spend time with the people who know you best. When you pray, remember how well God knows you. Nothing you say will surprise him, so tell God everything!

NO ONE CAN TAKE YOU OUT OF GOD'S HAND

You belong to Jesus, and since God is more powerful than anyone else, no one can kidnap you away from him. *John 10:27-30*

Footprint   The Jewish leaders, the Romans, and even the devil thought they had won when Jesus was crucified. But they could never take God's Son from him. It was all part of God's plan to make us his children too. *John 10:17-19 Story 177*

YOU ARE A FRIEND TO ME

VERSE 1

Elaine Osborne

I lay down my life.

I trust __ and o - bey, my God.

CHORUS

You are al - ways think - ing of me,

You are al - ways watch - ing me,

You are a friend __ to me. __

VERSE 2
I will live and breathe
In the presence of my Lord,
My God.

VERSE 3
You heal me
And fill my life with good things,
My God.

PART THREE
THE HOLY SPIRIT

YOU CAN RECEIVE THE GIFT OF THE HOLY SPIRIT

Jesus promised the gift of God's Holy Spirit to every Christian. If you are his child and a member of his family, then you have his Spirit living inside of you. The Holy Spirit will teach you what is true. *Luke 11:13 John 16:13 Acts 2:37-39*

Footprint Here are some accounts of people receiving the Holy Spirit: *Acts 2:1-4 / 8:14-17 / 10:44-48 / 19:1-7 Stories 179, 184*

64

THE COMFORTER

Jesus sent the Holy Spirit to teach you and to guide you into all truth. He will remind you of the things Jesus taught and even tell you about the future. He will speak to your hearts and lead you every day, helping you grow as a child of God. The Holy Spirit is also called the Comforter, and he will comfort you when you are lonely or afraid.
John 14:25-26 / 16:13-14 Romans 8:14

Footprint When you were younger did you have a special blanket or teddy bear to comfort you? Jesus promises us that the Comforter is with us to comfort us and to teach us. That's a promise to hang on to!

65

THE HOLY SPIRIT WILL PREPARE US FOR CHRIST

The Bible tells us that the church is Jesus' bride, and Jesus is the groom. The Holy Spirit has come to work in us to get us ready for Christ so that we may be the perfect bride for our perfect groom. *Ephesians 5:25-27*

Footprint   Ask your mom and dad to tell you about their wedding day. A lot of people worked very hard to make that day special. The Holy Spirit has been sent to do that in us too. Since he has come to make us perfect for Christ, what kinds of things might he be working on in you?

THE HOLY SPIRIT WILL GIVE YOU SPECIAL ABILITIES

God gives different gifts and abilities to his children. None of them are better than the others; they are all needed to get the job done. To some he gives the ability to give wise advice; others are good at studying and teaching. Some have special faith; and others have the power to heal, do miracles, prophesy, and preach. Some have the power to tell when it is Satan speaking instead of God; and others can speak in languages they don't know while someone else is able to translate. But in every case *God* gives the gifts, and *all* are needed to do his work. *1 Corinthians 12*

Footprint   The church is like the human body. We need many different parts to eat, walk, play, and work. The church needs every member with his unique ability to be successful here on earth.

WHO IS THE HOLY SPIRIT?

Jesus said, "If you love me and obey me, the Father will give you another Comforter, and he will never leave you. He is the Holy Spirit, the Spirit who leads you into all truth. He will come to you from the Father and will tell you all about me."

The Holy Spirit helps us with our daily problems and in our prayers. We don't even know what we should pray for, nor how to pray as we should; but the Holy Spirit prays for us. We know about these things because God has sent his Spirit to tell us, and his Spirit searches out and shows us all of God's deepest secrets. No one can know God's thoughts except God's own Spirit. And God has actually given us his Spirit to tell us about all the wonderful free gifts of grace and blessing that God has given us. You can never be lost to God's Spirit. If you go up to the heavens he is there; if you go down to the place of the dead he is there. If you ride in the morning winds to the farthest oceans, even there his hand will guide you and his strength will support you.

John 14:15-17 / 15:26 1 Corinthians 2:10-12 Psalm 139:6-10

PART FOUR
PRAYER

GOD HEARS YOUR PRAYERS

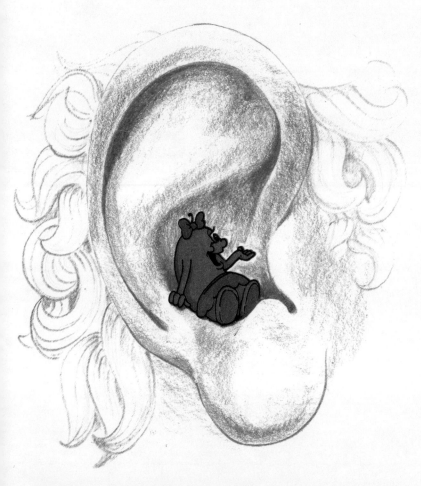

God is always listening to your prayers. And you can be sure that he will always answer them in the way that is best for you, even if you don't know what that best way is. *1 John 5:14-15*

Footprint   Hannah prayed and asked God for a son. Before she left the temple, she knew God had heard her. Soon she gave birth to a baby boy. *1 Samuel 1 Story 74*

GOD WILL GIVE YOU THE THINGS YOU ASK FOR

When we want things that are pleasing to God, we can ask for them and God will give them to us. He wants us to ask for things that honor him, not just things that make us happy.
Matthew 21:22 Mark 11:24 1 John 3:21-22

Footprint God spoke to Solomon in a dream and told him could have anything he wanted. Read *1 Kings 3* or *Story 96* to see what happened.

GOD WILL DO MORE THAN YOU ASK

Sometimes we pray only for things we can imagine or actually see. But God can work out every detail in your life and do more than you would ever dare to ask or even dream of.
Ephesians 3:20

Footprint   King Jehoshaphat asked for God's help because a great army was going to attack him. What happened was beyond what he hoped or prayed for.
2 Chronicles 20 Story 115

72

YOUR PRAYERS ARE POWERFUL

When you have a clean conscience and you ask God for something earnestly from your heart, your prayer has great power and will bring wonderful results. *James 5:16-17*

Footprint   Elijah was as completely human as you are, and yet when he prayed for food for a woman and her son, God answered his prayer. Read *Story 101 and 1 Kings 17:17-24* to discover another miracle that helped this woman and her son.

GOD ANSWERS YOU WHEN YOU CRY FOR HELP

Because God is your helper, you never need to be afraid.
Whenever you are faced with any kind of trouble, cry out to
God, and he will rescue you.
2 Chronicles 20:9 Psalm 46:1-2 Hebrews 13:6

Footprint   David was attacked once by a lion and
another time by a bear, and then he fought Goliath. Each time
he trusted God for help and won. *1 Samuel 17 Story 80*

74

GOD WILL HELP YOU
DESIRE RIGHT THINGS

If you make God your friend he will help you to want things that please him. Then you know what? When you ask for those things he will give them to you. *Psalms 21:2 / 37:4 / 145:9*

Footprint   Elisha desired something great, and God gave it to him. *2 Kings 2 Story 106*

GOD WILL HELP OTHERS WHEN YOU PRAY

Pray for others. Ask God to fix and to heal any part of their life that needs it. When you do, God will help them. Then you can thank God together for his wonderful answers to prayer.
2 Corinthians 1:11 Philippians 1:19 James 5:16

Footprint Job's problems began to turn around when he prayed for his friends. When you pray for others, God will help you as well. *Job 42:10*

PRAYING IN AGREEMENT

It is important for you to pray with other people. Jesus said, "If two of you agree in prayer down here on earth concerning anything you ask for, my Father in heaven will do it for you. For where two or three gather together because they are mine, I will be right there among them." *Matthew 18:19-20*

Footprint   One time when Peter and John and the other disciples prayed in agreement, they not only got what they prayed for but the whole building shook! *Acts 4:21-32*

THE HOLY SPIRIT WILL HELP YOU PRAY

When you don't know how to pray or even what you should pray for, the Holy Spirit will tell God what you really mean, even if you don't know how to say it. He prays with such feeling that it can't be expressed in words. But everything he prays is in harmony with God's will. *Romans 8:26-27*

Footprint   Do you ever get so excited about something or so mad about another thing that you can't explain it to anyone? Paul tells us that the Holy Spirit can put our feelings into words for us and help us communicate with God, who knows our hearts.

78

GOD WILL REWARD YOUR FAITH

Jesus said that if you had faith even as small as a tiny mustard seed, you could say to a mountain "Move!" and it would go away. Since God works for us, nothing can stand against us.
Matthew 17:20 Romans 8:31

Footprint   Question: What is faith? Answer: Hebrews 11:1. Read about "The Great Heroes of Faith" in the rest of *Hebrews 11.*

TEACH ME TO PRAY

When Jesus prayed the "Lord's Prayer," he was teaching you how to talk to God.

Our Father in heaven, we honor your holy name.

Talk to God, thanking him. Your faith is shown by your thankfulness, and God responds to faith.

We ask that your kingdom will come now.

Talk to God, putting his desire ahead of yours. His desire is for his kingdom to grow here on earth. When you put his kingdom first he'll take care of your desires.

May your will be done here on earth, just as it is in heaven.

Find out God's will in every situation and pray for that. If you pray according to his will, you know that he hears you.

Give us our food again today, as usual.

God already knows your daily needs. Just ask him, and he will make sure they are taken care of.

And forgive us our sins, just as we have forgiven those who have sinned against us.

Talk to God about your growth. Ask him to forgive your mistakes and to keep on changing you. Forgive and pray for the people who do wrong to you, and God will show them their mistakes and help them grow too.

Don't bring us into temptation, but deliver us from the Evil One.

Listen to the Holy Spirit. He'll show you the devil's plots against you so that you can destroy them with prayer before they ever reach you.

Another important thing to notice in this prayer is the words *our* and *we* and *us*, which tell you to pray these things for yourself and for others as well!

Amen.

Matthew 6:9-13

80

PART FIVE
WISDOM

GOD WILL GIVE YOU WISDOM FOR EVERY CIRCUMSTANCE

God can fill you with skill, ability, and knowledge in any area. He can give you great wisdom and understanding and a mind with broad interests. God is always ready to give you all the wisdom you need when you ask him for it.
Exodus 31:3 1 Kings 4:29 James 1:5

Footprint The wisdom that God gives is often not what you would have thought of yourself. Read the story of Gideon's army and see. *Judges 7 Story 65*

GOD WILL MAKE YOU WISE

Knowing God will help you understand many other things because he is the one who gives you wisdom. Every word from God is a treasure of knowledge and understanding; they fill your life with good things and make you wise.
Proverbs 2:6-8 / 9:10 Colossians 3:16

Footprint   Joseph wasn't one of Pharaoh's official wise men, but he was one of God's! Read how God provided Joseph with special wisdom at just the right time. *Genesis 39—41 Story 20*

You Can Know God's Will

The Holy Spirit will guide you and help you understand God's plan for your life and future. So don't brag about your plans. What you should say is, "If the Lord wants me to, I will do this or that." Since Jesus is your friend, he will guide you into the way God has for you.

John 15:15 / 16:13 Ephesians 5:10, 17 James 4:13-16

Footprint   Do people ask you what you want to be when you grow up? There is one answer that would always be true and would please God. You could tell people that you want to be whatever God wants you to be.

GOD WILL TEACH YOU

The Holy Spirit lives within you, and he will teach you every-thing you need to know. For God is glad to teach his ways to those who humbly turn to him. *Psalm 25:8-10 John 14:26 1 John 2:27*

Footprint   Be a smart apple like Baby 'Verb. Have a teachable heart.

WISDOM SPEAKS

"Listen to me!" Wisdom calls. "I have important information for you. Everything I say is right and true, for I hate lies and every kind of deception. My advice is wholesome and good. There is nothing of evil in it. My words are plain and clear to anyone with half a mind—if it is only open! My instruction is far more valuable than silver or gold.

"For the value of wisdom is far above rubies; nothing can be compared with it. Wisdom and good judgment live together, for wisdom knows where to discover knowledge and understanding. If anyone respects and fears God, he will hate evil. For wisdom hates pride, arrogance, corruption, and deceit of every kind.

"I, Wisdom, give good advice and common sense. Because of my strength, kings reign in power, and rulers make just laws. I love all who love me. Those who search for me shall surely find me. Unending riches, honor, justice, and righteousness are mine to distribute. My gifts are better than the purest gold or sterling silver! My paths are those of justice and right. Those who follow me are indeed wealthy. I fill their treasuries." *Proverbs 8:6-21*

PART SIX

SCHOOL

GOD WILL HELP YOU DO YOUR BEST IN SCHOOL

Wisdom is the main pursuit of sensible men. God can help you become wise and do your best in school. He will help you even with hard subjects, but you must first want to learn.
Job 32:8-9 Proverbs 17:16 Daniel 1:17 / 2:21-22

Footprint You can sleep your way through school but you won't become wise that way. Ask God to make you wise and give you a heart for truth, and then do your best to learn all that you can.

GOD WILL HELP YOU GET ALONG WITH YOUR TEACHERS

If you trust the Lord completely and never trust in your own ability to impress your teachers, God promises to bless you in your desire to learn from them. He will give your teachers a special appreciation for you which will help your education. *Proverbs 3:4-5 Daniel 1:9, 18-19*

Footprint Daniel and three of his friends went to school and did so well because they trusted God, that they became the king's counselors. *Daniel 1 Story 131*

DANIEL AT SCHOOL

King Nebuchadnezzar of Babylon ordered Ashpenaz, who was in charge of his palace personnel, to select some Jewish youths—young men of the royal family and nobility of Judah—and teach them the Chaldean language and literature. "Pick strong, healthy, good-looking lads," he said, "those who have read widely in many fields, are well informed, alert and sensible, and have enough poise to look good around the palace."

Daniel, Hananiah, Mishael, and Azariah were four of the many young men chosen. All four of them were from the tribe of Judah.

Daniel and his friends were very careful to please God and do everything that they knew was right, even though they were in a strange land.

So God gave their teachers a special appreciation for them. God also gave these four youths great ability to learn, and they soon mastered all the literature and science of the time.

They went to school for three years. Before they graduated the teacher brought all of the young men in the school to the king for exams.

King Nebuchadnezzar had long talks with each of them and none of them impressed him as much as Daniel, Hananiah, Mishael, and Azariah. So they were put on his regular staff of advisers. And in all matters requiring information and balanced judgment, the king found these young men's advice ten times better than that of all the wise men in his realm. *Daniel 1*

PART SEVEN
REWARDS

GOD REWARDS OBEDIENCE

If you love Jesus you will obey him. When you obey him, you will find that things turn out well for you, and God will bless you with all you need throughout your life.
Job 36:11 Jeremiah 42:6 John 14:21, 23

Footprint   As a soldier in the army you don't have to worry about clothes or food or shelter. Those things are provided for you as a reward for the job you are doing. When you are in God's army, taking care of what he wants done, he'll take care of your needs. *I Corinthians 9:7*

God Has Great Rewards for You

Make sure that you do what the Lord wants you to. For when you leave this life and enter heaven God will reward you for your obedience in ways that you can't imagine. You will live in the beautiful city of God and share in all of his glories. You will enjoy an unending glorious future.
Colossians 3:4 2 John 8 Revelation 2:10, 26 / 3:12, 21

Footprints   No mere man has ever seen, heard or even imagined what wonderful things God has ready for those who love the Lord. *1 Corinthians 2:9*

GOD GIVES YOU GOOD AND PERFECT THINGS

Whatever is good and perfect comes to you from God. The things he gives are good and perfect because he is good and perfect, and he will never change. *James 1:17*

Footprint If God is good and perfect why do so many bad things happen? It's the devil who is causing the stealing, killing and destroying in this world. Jesus came to defeat him so we could enjoy life in all its fullness. *John 10:10*

94

GOD WILL GIVE YOU THE BLESSINGS OF ABRAHAM

God told Abraham that he would bless him here on earth and that he would go to heaven because he believed God's promises. When you trust God, you will share the same blessings that Abraham received. *Galatians 3:6-9*

Footprint   Read *Genesis 13* or *Story 6*. What was most important to Lot? What about Abraham? Abraham trusted God and did the right thing. God blesses us when we trust him.

THE CROWN OF LIFE

You'll be happy it you don't give in and do wrong when you are tempted, for afterwards you will get as your reward the crown of life that God has promised those who love him. *James 3:11*

Footprint   When it comes to being a Christian you should be like an athlete. They deny themselves many things so that they can do their best. They go to all this trouble for a blue ribbon, but we do it for a heavenly reward that never disappears. *1 Corinthians 9:24-25 Story 203*

GOD REWARDS SACRIFICE

Sacrificing or even sharing isn't always easy, but Jesus said that if you give up anything to follow him, you will receive a hundred times as much in return here on earth, and in the world to come. *Matthew 19:29 Mark 10:29-30*

Footprint   The twelve disciples left everything to follow Jesus. Not only were they blessed in many ways while they were here on earth but Jesus promised each one that they would inherit eternal life as a reward for their sacrifice. *Matthew 19:27, 29*

RUNNING THE RACE

In a race, everyone runs, but only one person gets the prize. So run your race—the one God has you running in as a Christian—to win. To win the contest you must deny yourselves many things that would keep from doing your best. An athlete goes to all this trouble just to win a blue ribbon or a silver cup, but you do it for a heavenly reward that never disappears. So run straight to the goal of being all that God wants you to be. Have purpose in every step. Fight to win; don't just shadow box and play around. Like an athlete, train your body to do what it should, not what it wants to.

And remember that there is a huge crowd of people, people of faith, watching you from the grandstand of heaven.

So get rid of anything that slows you down or holds you back, especially those sins that wrap themselves so tightly around your feet and trip you up. And run with patience the particular race that God has set before you.

1 Corinthians 9:24-27 Hebrews 12:1

98

PART EIGHT

STAYING ON THE PATH

GOD WILL LOVINGLY CORRECT YOU

God will train and correct you, like a loving father corrects his children. He does it for your good so that you will become wise and have strong character. So don't be discouraged when God shows you where you are wrong. *Hebrews 12:5-11*

Footprint   God will keep on training and correcting you. Peter had been a leader in the church for many years when God used the Apostle Paul to correct him for something he was doing wrong. *Galatians 2:11-14*

100

GOD WILL DISCIPLINE YOU TO KEEP YOU ON THE RIGHT TRACK

If you don't listen to the Lord's teaching he will discipline you so that you won't end up in a real mess! God's discipline proves he loves you. For a loving father disciplines the children he loves in order to make them better.
Proverbs 3:11-12 1 Corinthians 11:32

Footprint In the same way that your parents have to discipline you to help you grow into a responsible and God-loving person, God promises to discipline you so that you will stay on the right path. *Proverbs 29:15, 17-19*

GOD WILL NEVER LEAVE YOU

When you became a Christian, God gave you a new heart. He wrote his ways in your heart and filled it with the desire to honor and follow him. Then God put his Spirit within you to give you the strength and ability to follow him. He promises that he will never leave you, and that he will always keep you near him. *Jeremiah 31:3, 33 Ezekiel 36:26-27*

Footprint   Peter probably felt like he had left Jesus for good after saying he didn't know him three times; but you can never leave God because God will never give up on you. He will always love you. *Luke 22:56-62 Story 174*

GOD WILL HELP YOU OBEY HIM

God is at work within you, helping you want to obey him, and then helping you do what he wants. He will make you pure and devoted and keep your spirit, soul and body strong.
Philippians 2:13 1 Thessalonians 5:23-24

Footprint You are stronger than Samson was, because the strength that really counts is the ability to obey God. As a Christian, God has given you all the strength you need to do what he wants you to. *Judges 16 Story 70*

GOD WILL FINISH HIS WORK IN YOU

When you first trusted God, he began to work in you to make you better and help you love him more. He will keep on helping you grow right up until the day you see Jesus face to face. *Philippians 1:6*

Footprint When God first spoke to Moses about leading the people of Israel, Moses told God he couldn't do it. But God worked in him and through him and in the end, he became one of Israel's great leaders. *Exodus 3 Story 29*

GOD WILL CAUSE YOU TO BECOME LIKE JESUS

From before you were born, God knew who you would be, and more than anything he wants you to be like Jesus, good and perfect in every way. *Romans 8:29 2 Corinthians 3:18*

Footprint   Jesus said, "Anyone who has seen me has seen the Father!" When we become more like Jesus, people will be able to see God in our lives. *John 14:9 / 17:22-23*

THE MAZE

Can you help Baby 'Verb find his way through the maze to Smiley?

PART NINE

GOD WILL KEEP YOU

GOD WILL KEEP YOU FROM WICKEDNESS

God will give you the sense to stay away from evil and to not hang around with sinners, who hate God and laugh at him. For those who love God will be loved and rewarded by him, but those who hate God will be destroyed.
Proverbs 2:11-13 Psalm 1

Footprint God told Abraham to leave his country, which was a wicked place, and go to another country. Because Abraham left that wicked land, God blessed him. You should stay away from people who do evil and get you into trouble. *Genesis 12 Story 6*

GOD WILL NOT TEMPT YOU

When you want to do wrong it is never God who is tempting you, for God never wants to do wrong and never tempts anyone else to do it. Temptation comes from your own bad thoughts and wishes. So watch out for bad thoughts because they lead to bad actions, and bad actions will ruin you.
Proverbs 4:23 James 1:13-14

Footprint Temptation is always full of lies. When the devil tempted Jesus, Jesus quoted Scripture to fight those lies. Remember God's Word when you have wrong thoughts and temptations. *Matthew 4:1-11*

GOD WILL SHOW YOU HOW TO ESCAPE TEMPTATION'S POWER

No temptation is too strong to resist. You can trust God to keep the temptation from becoming so strong that you can't stand up against it, for he has promised this and he will do what he says. He will show you how to escape temptation's power so that you can do what's right. *1 Corinthians 10:13*

Footprint   The Lord rescued Lot out of the wicked city of Sodom because he was a good man. God will also rescue you from the temptations that surround you if you will read his Word and try to obey and love him. *Genesis 19 2 Peter 2:7-9 Story 8*

THE HOLY SPIRIT WILL HELP YOU AVOID TEMPTATION

Sometimes the Holy Spirit speaks to you through your conscience. When your conscience tells you that you have done something wrong, listen to it. The Holy Spirit will help you know how to do what is right. *Galatians 5:16, 25*

Footprint Before Adam and Eve ate the forbidden fruit in the Garden of Eden, their conscience told them what they ought to do. But they didn't obey God or listen to their conscience. What happened because they didn't listen? *Genesis 3:2*

GOD HAS DESTROYED
SIN'S POWER OVER YOU

Even though you still sin, when you became a Christian the part of you that *wanted* to sin was taken away and crushed. So don't even answer when sin calls; give yourself completely to God instead. *Romans 6:2-13*

Footprint   After Jesus went to heaven, some wonderful and amazing things happened to the disciples and others who gave themselves to God. Read about it in *Acts 2:40-47*.

112

THE HOLY SPIRIT WILL PRODUCE FRUIT IN YOU

When you let the Holy Spirit control your life, he will produce this kind of fruit in you: love, joy, peace, patience, kindness, goodness, faithfulness, gentleness and self control.
Galatians 5:19-23

Footprint   Stephen was so full of God's fruit and love that he asked God to forgive the men who were killing him!
Acts 6:5-15 / 7:54-60 Story 181

GOD'S KIND OF PERSON

Oh, the joys of those who do not follow evil men's advice, who do not hang around with sinners, scoffing at the things of God. But they delight in doing everything God wants them to, and day and night are always meditating on his word and thinking about ways to follow him more closely.

They are like trees along a river bank bearing luscious fruit each season without fail. Their leaves shall not wither, and all they do shall prosper.

But for sinners, what a different story! They blow away like chaff before the wind. They are not safe on Judgment Day; they shall not stand among the godly.

For the Lord watches over all the plans and paths of godly men, but the paths of the godless lead to doom.

Psalm 1

PART TEN
FORGIVE-
NESS

GOD HAS GIVEN YOU HIS RIGHTEOUSNESS

When you put your faith and trust in Christ to save you, God makes you ready for heaven by forgiving your sins. Then he makes you right in his sight, by filling you with his own goodness. *Romans 1:17 2 Corinthians 5:21*

Footprint   God does not call you righteous because of the good things you do as a Christian. You are always perfect in God's sight because he has forgiven and forgotten all of your sins. It's a free gift! *Galatians 3:2-3 Romans 1:17 Story 199*

GOD HAS WASHED YOU TOTALLY CLEAN

When you become a Christian every sin you have ever committed, known or unknown, is washed away. No matter how deep the stain of your sin is, God makes you as clean as freshly fallen snow. *Isaiah 1:18 1 Corinthians 6:11*

Footprint In the Old Testament, before a priest could go into the tabernacle where God's presence was, he had to wash first. Jesus washes you with the pure water of his forgiveness and now you are always ready to spend time with God. *Exodus 40:12 Hebrews 10:22 Story 40*

GOD HAS FORGOTTEN YOUR SINS

God not only forgives your sins, but he forgets them too. He throws them into the depths of the ocean and promises never to think of them again. *Isaiah 43:25 Jeremiah 31:34 Micah 7:19*

Footprint   Once you have asked God to forgive you, forgive yourself then forget it. How far is the east from the west? That is how far God takes our sin away from us. *Psalm 103:2*

118

GOD IS MAKING YOU HOLY

When you became a Christian God said that he would make you holy. So God sees you as perfect, then he begins to work within you and help you to grow so that in the end, you will be perfect.

John 17:19 Romans 6:22 Hebrews 10:14 / 12:10 1 Peter 1:14-16 / 2:9

Footprint The apostle Peter did miracles, became a great leader in the church, and wrote part of the Bible. But do you remember some of the mistakes he made when God first started working on him?

Matthew 14:23-32 / 26:69-75 Mark 8:31-33 Story 174

YOU DON'T EVER HAVE TO FEEL ACCUSED OR CONDEMNED

If God has chosen you to be his child, who can tell you that you're not? Nobody! Jesus died for you, and he will be on your side when others make fun of you for obeying God. *Romans 8:33-34*

Footprint   Gideon didn't think very much of himself, but God called him a "Mighty Soldier." Read and find out which is right, God's opinion of someone or their own opinion of themselves. *Judges 6–7 Story 65*

God Will Help You Forgive Others

Though it may sound hard, forgiving others is easier when you remember that God forgives them and loves them just as he loves you. He promises you his strength to do it.
Ephesians 4:32 1 John 5:4

Footprint   Peter came to Jesus and asked, "Sir, how often should I forgive a brother who sins against me? Seven times?" Jesus answered, "No! Seventy times seven!" In other words, there is never a time when God doesn't want you to forgive. *Matthew 18:21-35 Story 162*

GOD ALWAYS GIVES YOU ANOTHER CHANCE

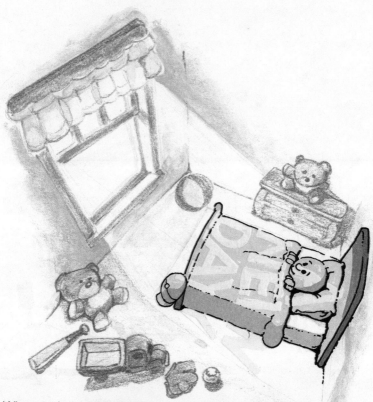

When you don't measure up to everything that you feel you should be, remember that God loves you just as you are. Because of his love, you can have a fresh start each day. So forget the past, and look forward to what lies ahead. For anyone who confesses their mistakes gets another chance.
Proverbs 28:13 Lamentations 3:21-23 Philippians 3:13

Footprint   King David made just as many mistakes as King Saul. But Saul tried to justify himself while David admitted his mistakes and asked God to forgive him. *1 Samuel 15 Psalm 41:4 Story 79*

122

GOD WILL FORGIVE YOU WHEN YOU SIN

If you confess your sins to God, you can depend on him to forgive you and cleanse you from every wrong. For Jesus died to wash away all your sins, even the ones that happened before you knew who God was. *1 John 1:9*

Footprint   When Jonah wouldn't do what God wanted him to, God made a great fish swallow him. Jonah sat in that fish for three days and thought about his sin. But when Jonah confessed his sin and agreed to follow God, God rescued him. *Jonah 1–2 Story 73*

FORGIVE AND BE FORGIVEN

Jesus told this story: "There was a king," he said, "and a man who owed the king a million dollars. Since the man couldn't pay back all that money, the king ordered him and his wife and his children to be sold as slaves. The money they were sold for would be paid to the king for the debt. That was the custom in those days. Then the man fell down on his knees before the king and begged him to be patient until he could repay the money. The king was sorry for him and was kind—he forgave him the entire debt!

"But that same man went out and found another man who owed him only a few dollars. He caught him by the throat and said, 'Pay me what you owe me!' The man fell down at his feet and begged, 'Have patience with me and I will pay back everything I owe you.' But the first man wouldn't wait; he had him arrested and thrown into jail, to be kept there until he paid.

"When the king heard about this he sent for the first man. 'How low can a man get?' he demanded. 'I forgave you all that huge debt just because you asked me to, and shouldn't you have pitied that other fellow just as I pitied you?' And the angry king sent him away to be punished until he paid back all he owed."

In this story the king means God and the man who owed so much means you. When you became a Christian God forgave you a great debt, all your sins. Now he expects you to forgive others in the same way. *Matthew 18:21-35 Story 162*

PART ELEVEN
TRUTH

GOD WILL LEAD YOU INTO ALL TRUTH

The Holy Spirit is the source of everything that is true. Most people don't know him because they aren't looking for truth. But you are; so the Holy Spirit inside you helps you understand all that is true. *John 14:17 / 15:26 / 16:13*

Footprint When Pilate asked Jesus, "What is truth?" he probably wouldn't have been able to understand Jesus' answer. Only Christians can understand God's truth. *John 18:37-38 2 Thessalonians 2:10-11*

GOD IS TRUTH

God doesn't lie or change his mind like humans do. You can be perfectly sure that he will always do what he says he'll do, so you can count on him completely.
Numbers 23:18-24 John 3:33-34 Hebrew 6:17-18

Footprint   When you ask God for something he has promised, be sure that you really expect him to do it. For when you doubt, it's like saying that you don't believe God can do it. Believe in what you ask for. *James 1:6-8*

TELL THE TRUTH

Whatever is true will always be true, but lies can never last. Telling lies will get you into trouble. Telling the truth will make you happy and cause everyone to respect your words.
Proverbs 12:13-14, 19 / 21:28

Footprint   When Ananias and Sapphira lied to Peter, Peter said that they had lied to God! Read and see what happened. *Acts 5 Story 180*

YOU CAN RECOGNIZE THE TRUTH

You don't have to believe everything you hear just because someone says God told them so: test it first to see if it really is. Does it really agree with everything the Bible says? If not, the message is not from God. *1 John 4:1-3*

Footprint   You can read about some Christians who listened to false teachers in the book of Galatians. *Story 199*

TELLING THE TRUTH

Lies will get anyone into trouble, but honesty is its own defense.

Truth stands the test of time; lies are quickly exposed.

Honesty will guide you; dishonesty will destroy you.

The good hate lies; the wicked lie constantly and come to shame.

No one believes someone who lies, but everyone respects the words of someone who always tells the truth.

Telling the truth will bring you great satisfaction.
Proverbs 12:13, 19 / 11:3 / 13:5 / 21:28 / 12:14

PART TWELVE

YOUR FUTURE

THE HOLY SPIRIT WILL TELL YOU ABOUT THE FUTURE

When the Holy Spirit comes he will guide you into everything that is true, for he will not be telling his own ideas, but will be passing along to you what he has heard straight from God.
John 16:13

Footprint   Have you had to make a hard decision and wished that God would just write the answer on the wall for you? God doesn't usually do things like that, but he does promise that the Holy Spirit will guide you if you ask him to. Trust God with your toughest questions about the future.

GOD HAS A PLAN FOR YOUR LIFE

God has planned your path in life ahead of you. He'll even tell you where to stop and rest. He saw you before you were born and knew what each day of your life would be like. Every day of yours is special to him. *Psalm 139:3, 16*

Footprint   Before you were born, God knew you. And only he knows your future. So when you're making plans for the future say, "If the Lord wants me to, I'll do this or that." *James 4:13-16*

GOD WILL CAUSE YOUR HOPES AND DREAMS TO COME TRUE

When you ask God to answer your prayers, he may not give you what you ask for, but his answers will always go beyond your wildest dreams. God wants what is best for you.
Psalm 65 / 145:19

Footprint   When God says, "I'll give you all your heart's desires," he is saying that he will put the right desires in your heart and that he'll fulfill those desires. And God cares about the little things in your life, not just the big ones. *Psalm 37:4-5*

GOD HAS A GREAT FUTURE FOR YOU

When you allow God to make you wise, a bright and wonderful future lies ahead of you. As others see your future unfold they'll know that there is a God who rewards those who love him. *Psalm 58:11 Proverbs 23:17-18 / 24:13-14*

Footprint   In *The Book* there are many examples of people who could never have dreamed or imagined the future God had planned for them. Can you name a few? *Stories 19, 28, 49, 80*

GOD KNOWS YOUR FUTURE

O Lord, you have examined my heart and know everything about me. You know when I sit or stand. When far away you know my every thought. You chart the path ahead of me, and tell me where to stop and rest.

Every moment, you know where I am. You know what I am going to say before I even say it. You both precede me and follow me, and place your hand of blessing on my head.

You made all the delicate, inner parts of my body, and knit them together in my mother's womb. Thank you for making me so wonderfully complex! It is amazing to think about. Your workmanship is marvelous — and how well I know it. You were there while I was being formed in utter seclusion! You saw me before I was born and scheduled each day of my life before I began to breathe. Every day was recorded in your Book!

How precious it is, Lord, to realize that you are thinking about me constantly! I can't even count how many times a day your thoughts turn towards me. And when I waken in the morning, you are still thinking of me!

Search me, O God, and know my heart; test my thoughts. Point out anything you find in me that makes you sad, and lead me along the path of everlasting life.

Psalm 139:1-5, 13-18, 23-24

PART THIRTEEN
HEART AND SOUL

GOD WILL GIVE YOU PEACE OF HEART AND MIND

Don't worry about anything; instead pray about everything. If you do this you will experience God's peace, which is far more wonderful than the human mind can understand. His peace will keep your thoughts and your hearts quiet and at rest as you trust in Christ. *Philippians 4:6-7*

Footprint   The peace that the people in the world have is fragile because it depends on the things that are happening around them. But the peace that Jesus gives isn't affected by trials and problems. It's always there. *John 14:27 / 16:33*

GOD'S WORDS WILL HELP CONTROL YOUR THOUGHTS

Keep a close watch on everything you think. Run from anything that gives you evil thoughts, and fill your mind with God's words instead. For when God's words are stored in your heart they will steer your thoughts and hold you back from sin. *Psalm 119:11 Colossians 3:2 1 Timothy 4:16 2 Timothy 2:22*

Footprint   It's important to spend your time with others who love the Lord. For you will become like the people you spend time with. *Proverbs 13:20 2 Timothy 2:22*

139

GOD WILL HELP YOU HAVE THE ATTITUDE OF CHRIST

God gives patience, steadiness, and encouragement to help you live at peace with other people. How can you do that? Don't be selfish; don't live to make a good impression on others. Be humble, thinking of others as better than yourself. Don't just think about your own affairs, but be interested in others, too. *Romans 15:5 Philippians 2:3-8*

Footprint Jesus always had the right attitude. He was God, but he served others. Do you remember the time he surprised everyone by doing a slave's job? Read *Story 172 John 13*.

GOD WILL GIVE YOU HIS NATURE

When you become a Christian you become a brand new person inside. God gave you his nature, his own character. As you clothe yourself with this new nature, your attitudes and thoughts will be constantly changing for the better.

Romans 1:4-5 / 6:2-4 2 Corinthians 6:17 Ephesians 4:23-24 2 Peter 1:4

Footprint   When Jesus was betrayed his clothes and his life were taken away. But because of his betrayal and death he is able to clothe anyone who comes to him with the new clothes of God's nature. Does this remind you of a story in *The Book? Genesis 37, 45 Stories 19, 25*

Words of Peace

He will keep in perfect peace all those who trust in him, whose thoughts turn often to the Lord! *Isaiah 26:3*

Jesus said, "I am leaving you with a gift—peace of mind and heart! And the peace I give isn't fragile like the peace the world gives. So don't be troubled or afraid." *John 14:27*

Jesus said, "I have told you all this so that you will have peace of heart and mind." *John 16:33*

May all God's mercies and peace be yours from God our Father and from Jesus Christ our Lord. *Romans 1:6-7*

Don't worry about anything; instead, pray about everything; tell God your needs and don't forget to thank him for his answers. If you do this you will experience God's peace, which is far more wonderful than the human mind can understand. His peace will keep your thoughts and your hearts quiet and at rest as you trust in Christ Jesus. *Philippians 4:6-7*

Let the peace of heart which comes from Christ be always present in your hearts and lives, for this is your responsibility and privilege as members of his body. And always be thankful. *Colossians 3:15*

PART FOURTEEN

TALENT AND ABILITY

GOD WILL HELP YOU DO THINGS WELL

Happy is the person who has God as their helper. In everything you do, put God first and he will direct you and crown your efforts with success. And as you use the strength, wisdom, and energy that God supplies people will be able to see him working in you.

Psalm 146:5 Proverbs 3:4-6 2 Corinthians 3:5 / 12:9 1 Peter 4:11

Footprint Paul said, "I am glad to boast about how weak I am; I am glad to be a living demonstration of Christ's power, instead of showing off my own power and abilities." Are you weak in some areas? Let God be strong in those areas and remember to give him the credit when you succeed.
2 Corinthians 12:9

144

GOD WILL HELP YOU IMPROVE THE TALENTS HE HAS GIVEN YOU

Put the abilities that God has given you to work; throw yourself into your tasks so that everyone may notice your improvement and progress. God rejoices when you know what you're doing. But remember you're not doing it on your own.
Proverbs 14:35 Romans 12:6 2 Corinthians 3:5 1 Timothy 4:15

Footprint God expects us to use the abilities he gives us and improve them. Read the story Jesus told about the man who gave his servants some money to use to earn more for him. *Matthew 25 Story 170*

GOD GIVES EACH ONE OF US DIFFERENT ABILITIES

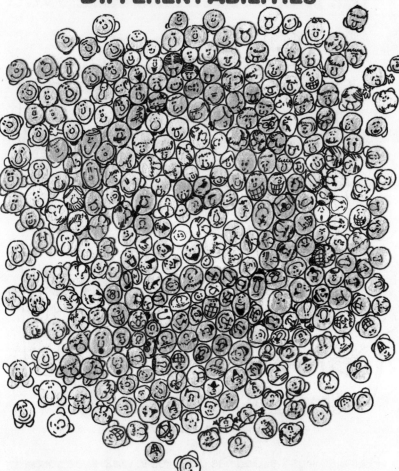

God has given you some special abilities. Be sure to use them to help others. For we are all in the same family. *1 Corinthians 12:27 Ephesians 4:7 1 Peter 4:10*

Footprint Just as your hands do one kind of job and your ears do something entirely different, each Christian is one special part of the "body" of Jesus Christ. What part of the "body" are you? *1 Corinthians 12:12-27 Story 198*

146

God Has Given You Spiritual Gifts

God always has shown that his messages are true by signs and wonders and various miracles and by giving certain special abilities from the Holy Spirit to those who believe. Yes, God has given special gifts to you, too. *Hebrews 2:4*

Footprint   Paul told his young friend Timothy to pay attention to and practice the God-given ability he had received as a gift from the Holy Spirit. Ask God to help you strengthen your gifts too. *2 Timothy 1:14*

147

SPECIAL ABILITIES FOR THE CHURCH

All of you together are the one body of Christ, and each one of you is a separate and necessary part of it. Here is a list of some of the parts he has placed in his church, which is his body.

- the ability to be an apostle
- the ability to be a prophet
- the ability to teach others
- the ability to preach well
- the special ability for winning people to Christ
- the ability to care for God's people like a shepherd with his sheep
- the ability to do miracles
- the ability to heal
- the ability to help others
- the ability to get others to work together easily
- the ability to speak in different kinds of languages
- the ability to be generous
- the ability to lead and get things done
- the ability to comfort others

Romans 12:6-8 1 Corinthians 12:27-28 Ephesians 4:11

PART FIFTEEN
WORDS

GOD WILL HELP YOU GUARD WHAT YOU SAY

The Holy Spirit gives you self-control and part of self-control is controlling your tongue. Ask the Lord to help you keep your lips sealed until you have thought through what you have to say. *Psalm 141:3 Proverbs 13:3 / 15:38 Galatians 5:23*

Footprint Say only what is good and helpful to those you are talking to and what will give them a blessing.
Ephesians 4:29

GOD WILL GIVE YOU THE RIGHT THING TO SAY

How wonderful it is when God gives you the right thing to say at the right time. When God's words fill your mouth, your words will make things calm and peaceful.
Psalm 81:10 Proverbs 12:18 / 15:23 / 16:23 Luke 21:15

Footprint   Sometimes it's hard to know what to say to someone who is suffering or needs encouragement. Ask God to give you just the right words. *2 Corinthians 1:3-7*

WHAT YOU SAY CAN HAPPEN IF YOU BELIEVE IT

Jesus said, "If you only have faith in God you can say to this mountain 'Rise up and fall into the sea', and your command will be obeyed. All that's required is that you really believe and have no doubt!" *Mark 11:22-23*

Footprint Not many of us have the kind of faith that Jesus had, but he wanted to show us how powerful faith can be. When he told his dead friend, Lazarus, to come out of the grave, Jesus had great faith. Read *John 11* and *Story 165* to find out just how powerful words spoken with great faith can be.

YOU CAN STEER YOUR LIFE

If you can control your tongue, you will have perfect control over yourself in every way. A tiny rudder makes a huge ship turn wherever the pilot wants it to go, even though the winds are so strong. In the same way what you say will affect your whole life. *James 3:1-12*

Footprint   On Judgment Day you must answer for every idle word you speak. Your words affect your life now and forever. So think before you speak!
Matthew 12:36-37 Story 205

153

Words of Wisdom

There is living truth in what a good person says.

When a good person speaks, he is worth listening to.

A good person speaks what is helpful.

The words of a wise person soothe and heal.

A wise person doesn't display his knowledge.

A word of encouragement does wonders.

A gentle answer turns away anger.

Gentle words cause life and health.

The Lord delights in kind words.

A good person thinks before he speaks.

Kind words are like honey—enjoyable and healthful.

A person of few words and a settled mind is wise.

A wise person's words express deep streams of thought.

Everyone respects the words of an honest person.

Let your words be wise, and kindness the rule for everything
you say!
*Proverbs 10:11, 20, 32 / 12:18, 23, 25 / 15:1, 4, 26, 28 / 16:24 / 17:27-28 /
18:4 / 21:28 / 31:26*

PART SIXTEEN
SALVATION

YOU ARE A MEMBER OF GOD'S FAMILY

When you trusted God to save you, he adopted you into his family. Now he is your Father and Jesus is your brother. Since you are God's child, what God has is yours too!
John 1:11-12 Galatians 4:5-7 Hebrews 2:11 1 Peter 1:3

Footprint You should take your rights as a member of God's family seriously. Remember the story about Esau's terrible mistake? *Genesis 24 Story 13*

YOU WILL LIVE FOREVER

God has given you eternal life. Yes, you will have forever all the wonders and wealth that he has promised you. But the best part of eternal life is that you will be with the Lord himself forever. And that's something to eagerly look forward to.
1 Thessalonians 4:17 Titus 3:7 Hebrews 9:15

Footprint   Read about "The New Jerusalem" where you'll be spending eternity with the Lord. *Revelation 21–22 Story 206*

YOU WILL GO TO HEAVEN

Jesus said, "There are many homes up there where my Father lives, and I am going to prepare them for your coming." So look forward to the joys of heaven! For when everything is ready, Jesus will come and get you, so that you can be with him where he is. *John 14:2 Colossians 1:5*

Footprint There is only one way to be sure that you are headed for heaven. Read *Story 150* and *John 3* to make sure you know the way.

158

YOU WILL KNOW THAT YOU ARE SAVED

There are two ways that you can know that you are saved.
First, God tells you in the Bible that if you ask him to save you,
he will certainly do it, no questions asked. Then, once you
have asked God to save you, the Holy Spirit will live inside
you and assure you that you are God's child.
Romans 8:16 1 John 5:13

Footprint   The reverse of this promise is also true. You
can know that you are not born again if you have not asked
God to save you. Read *Romans 10:9-10.*

GOD HAS GIVEN YOU A NEW LIFE

When you become a Christian, you become a brand new person inside. You have the chance to start all over again; but this time you are able to do things differently because God is always with you, helping you live the right way.

John 3:6 Romans 6:4 2 Corinthians 5:17

Footprint Something to think about: Paul said, "I myself no longer live, but Christ lives in me." Paul's life changed dramatically when God gave him a new one. Read *Stories 182–183* to learn more about this dramatic change.

YOU ARE A CITIZEN OF HEAVEN

Now you are no longer strangers to God and foreigners to heaven, but you are members of God's own family, citizens of God's country. And you belong in God's household with every other Christian. *Ephesians 2:19*

Footprint There are many different countries in the world and there are Christians in every one of those countries. Even though we all have different citizenship and look different and speak different languages, we are members of God's family and fellow citizens of his kingdom. *Hebrews 1:8-10 Story 6*

BORN AGAIN

After dark one night a Jewish religious leader named Nicodemus came to talk with Jesus.

"Sir," he said, "we all know that God has sent you to teach us. Your miracles are proof enough of this."

Jesus replied, "With all the earnestness I possess I tell you this: Unless you are born again, you can never get into the Kingdom of God."

"Born again!" exclaimed Nicodemus. "What do you mean? How can an old man go back into his mother's womb and be born again?"

Jesus replied, "What I am telling you so earnestly is this: Unless a person hears and accepts the Good News of me dying for their sins, and becomes eager to follow God's will, asking me to take away their sins and give them a brand new life, they cannot enter the kingdom of God. Humans can only have human babies, but the Holy Spirit gives birth to spiritual babies by giving you a brand new life from heaven; so don't be surprised at my statement that you must be born again!"

"What do you mean?" Nicodemus asked.

Jesus replied, "God loved the world so much that he gave his only Son so that anyone who believes in him shall not perish, but will be born again into an eternal life!" *John 3*

PART SEVENTEEN
SAFE AND SECURE

GOD WILL KEEP YOU FROM HARM

No real harm will come to you. Even though your body may get hurt your heart and soul are safe because God is your shield, protecting you and guarding your pathway.
Psalm 91:10 Proverbs 2:7-8 / 12:21 / 19:23

Footprint   Do you remember the story of Daniel and the lions' den? God can provide the same kind of protection for you. *Daniel 6 Story 135*

GOD WILL PROTECT YOUR HOUSE

My people will live in safety, quietly at home. *Isaiah 32:18*

Footprint   The Israelis' homes were protected from the terrible punishments that were sent on the Egyptians. God can protect your home and your things just as he protects you. If he takes things away from you, remember that they are really his anyway, and he only takes things away so that he can give us things that are better for us later. *Exodus 9:23-26 Story 32*

GOD IS YOUR SECURITY

The Lord is like a strong fortress or a high tower. When you trust him he becomes your place of safety. When you run to him no evil can reach you. *Proverbs 18:10 Psalm 18:2-3 / 91:2-3*

Footprint Unless the Lord is your protection, you aren't safe. Even the strongest fortresses can't always protect people who won't trust God. Remember the story of Jericho? *Psalm 127:1 Joshua 6 Story 167*

GOD IS ON YOUR SIDE

God is for you! You never need to be afraid. For if God is on your side, helping you, who can ever be against you?
Psalm 118:6-7 Romans 8:31

Footprint   One of Jesus' names is "Emmanuel" which means "God is with us." Isn't is nice to know that no matter what you encounter God is with you? *Matthew 1:23*

GOD WILL MAKE YOU
UNAFRAID OF WILD ANIMALS

When you trust God to make you safe, you won't need to worry about dangerous animals because God is caring for you like a mother cares for her babies.
Job 5:22-23 Ezekiel 34:25

Footprint   God can make animals do what he wants them to. Read *Daniel 6* to see how God controlled the lions. Read *Numbers 22 Story 52 for another great example.*

GOD WILL KEEP YOU SAFE FROM DISASTER

God will rescue you from danger. You don't need to be afraid of accidents that might happen during the day, or the evil things in the darkness, or even disasters that happen suddenly. For God is your shelter. *Psalm 91:2-6 Proverbs 10:25 / 11:8*

Footprint What was the biggest disaster that ever happened? You can read about it and how God saved the people who trusted in him. *Genesis 7 Story 4*

GOD WILL STICK UP FOR YOU

When others accuse you falsely or tell lies about you, God will stick up for you. He will show everyone that you are not guilty by making your work succeed and by bringing out the truth. So don't repay evil for evil, wait for the Lord to handle the matter. *Psam 9:3-4 Proverbs 20:22 Isaiah 54:17*

Footprint Aaron and Miriam were complaining about Moses, and God came to his defense. All you need to do is obey and love God, he'll take care of the rest. *Numbers 12 Story 48*

GOD'S ARMOR IS YOURS TO WEAR

God has given you his armor to use so that you can resist
Satan's attacks: The strong belt of truth and the breastplate of
God's approval; shoes that are able to speed you on as you
tell others the Good News of peace with God; faith as your
shield to stop the fiery arrows aimed at you by Satan; the
helmet of salvation; and the sword of the Spirit, which is the
word of God. *Ephesians 6:10-17*

Footprint   When David went out to kill Goliath the only
armor he wore was God's armor of faith. *1 Samuel 17:38-39
Story 80*

GOD'S WEAPONS ARE YOURS TO USE

God has given you mighty weapons that aren't like the ones made by men; they are stronger. God has given the weapons of prayer, love and courage to you so that you can knock down the devil's strongholds of fear and hate and darkness.
2 Corinthians 6:7 / 10:4-5

Footprint   Once Daniel prayed and fasted for three weeks. Then an angel came and told him that it took three weeks to get there because an evil spirit blocked his way. It was Daniel's prayer that helped him break through. Is there anything you could be praying about right now? *Daniel 10*

GOD WILL FIGHT YOUR BATTLES FOR YOU

Don't be stopped by any obstacle or problem that threatens you. The battle is not yours, but God's! Prepare to meet the problem, but remember, it's God who will conquer it for you. *2 Chronicles 20:15 Psalm 20:6-8 / 35:1*

Footprint   When the Assyrians came out to conquer Jerusalem, the Angel of the Lord went into their camp at night and killed 185,000 soldiers. Trust God to stand with you during all the battles that come your way. *Isaiah 37:33-38*

GOD RESCUES AND PROTECTS

You live in the shadow of the Almighty, sheltered by the God who is above all gods.

He is your fortress, your place of safety; he is your God, trust him. For he rescues you from every trap and protects you from deadly diseases. He will shield you with his wings. His faithful promises are your armor. Now you don't need to be afraid of the dark, nor accidents, nor evil things, not even disasters. For Jehovah is your protection! How then can evil overtake you or any evil come near? For he orders his angels to protect you wherever you go. They will steady you with their hands to keep you from stumbling.

For the Lord says, "Because you love me, I will rescue you; I will make you great because you trust in my name. When you call on me I will answer; I will be with you in trouble, and rescue you and honor you. I will satisfy you with a full life then bring you home to heaven." *Psalm 91:1-5, 9-16*

PART EIGHTEEN
THE DEVIL

GOD WILL RESCUE YOU FROM SATAN'S ATTACKS

Be careful! Watch out for attacks from Satan, your great enemy. Stand firm when he brings trouble into your life. God has promised to come and pick you up and make you stronger than ever. *2 Peter 5:8-10*

Footprint *Job 1* tells us that Satan was roaming the earth looking for someone to attack. God knew Job was strong, so he allowed Satan to attack Job. Do you like stories with happy endings? Read *Story 72* to find out how Job, with God's help, stood up under attack.

JESUS HAS DEFEATED SATAN

Jesus came to destroy the works of the devil. When Jesus died he went down to hell and broke Satan's power. He took the keys to hell and death, and rescued you out of the darkness of Satan's kingdom and brought you into his Kingdom of light.

Ephesians 4:8-9 Colossians 1:13 Hebrews 2:14 1 John 3:8 Revelation 1:18

Footprint Jesus' defeat of Satan is final. You can rest in the assurance that God is always in control.

WHEN YOU RESIST THE DEVIL HE WILL FLEE

You resist the devil when you obey and draw close to God, for then God will come closer to you. Example: When you stay angry with someone you give Satan a big foothold in your life, but if you obey God and always forgive, then you will have outsmarted and resisted the devil.

2 Corinthians 2:11 Ephesians 4:26-27 James 4:7-8

Footprint   When Satan tried to get Jesus to disobey God, Jesus resisted him by quoting from the Scripture. Maybe you could memorize some of God's promises to help you resist Satan. *Matthew 4:1-11 Story 149*

THE NAME OF JESUS

God put Jesus in charge of everything. So when you pray "In Jesus' name" it's as if God said it himself! He will do what you ask if you are asking for something that Jesus would want.
Mark 16:17 Luke 10:19 John 14:14 1 Corinthians 15:27 Philippians 2:9-10

Footprint   Jesus said that we could ask anything in his name and he would do it. When you feel Satan tempting you, stand firm and pray that Satan would run away from you. The power of Jesus will give you complete victory over Satan's temptation.

WHO IS SATAN?

When God created the devil he didn't create him evil. He was a beautiful angel. His name was "Lucifer, son of the morning."

God said that Lucifer was the perfection of wisdom and beauty. His clothing was covered with every precious stone—all in beautiful settings of gold.

God created him and gave him a special job; he had access to God's holy presence.

But his heart became filled with pride because of all his beauty and power. He said to himself, "I will go up to heaven and rule the angels. I will take God's highest throne!"

So God cast Lucifer out of his presence, along with one third of the angels that had followed Lucifer. These fallen angels, who are evil spirits, are still under the command of Lucifer (Satan).

When God created Adam and Eve, Satan tricked them into disobeying God and obeying him instead. By sinning and obeying Satan, these first people made him the god of this world.

When Jesus died for our sins he defeated Satan and gave everyone back the opportunity to choose who to serve as their God.

When Jesus comes back Satan will finally be locked away in hell, which was created for him and his angels. Then he will never be able to bother anyone again.

Genesis 3 Isaiah 14:12-15 Ezekiel 10 / 28:12-19 Luke 4:5-8 1 Corinthians 15:21-22 2 Corinthians 4:4 Ephesians 6:11-12 Revelation 12:3-4, 7-9

PART NINETEEN
ANGELS

GOD'S ANGELS WILL PROTECT YOU

God has ordered his angels to protect you. Wherever you go, you are watched and cared for. Nothing can happen to you that God does not know about because his angels are always standing guard over you. *Psalm 34:6-7 / 91:10-12*

Footprint   Once when Jesus was talking about children, he said, "I tell you that in heaven their angels have constant access to my Father." So be confident; your angels are on guard. *Matthew 18:10*

GOD'S ANGELS BRING GOD'S WILL TO PASS IN YOUR LIFE

Angels are God's messengers sent out to help and care for you and all other Christians. They listen for God's commands and then carry out his will in your life. *Psalm 103:20 Hebrews 1:17*

Footprint   Read *Acts 12* and *Story 185* to find out about one angel's rescue mission. You may never need the kind of help Peter needed, but the angels will be there for you no matter what.

SERVANTS OF GOD

Strong and mighty,
   servants of God.
Sent to protect you
   and keep you from harm.

Invisible but real,
   always around you.
Using their hands
   to cushion your path.

Gentle and kind,
   from babies they're with you.
Watching and listening,
   extending God's care.

Hearing God's orders
   they do what you've prayed.
Shaping his promises
   in your life every day.

Psalm 91:11-12 / 103:20-21 Hebrews 1:14

PART TWENTY
YOUR FAMILY

GOD WILL BLESS YOU
IF YOU OBEY YOUR PARENTS

Obey your parents; this is the right thing to do because God has placed them in authority over you. Honor your father and mother. This is the first of God's Ten Commandments that ends with a promise. And this is the promise: if you honor your father and mother, you will have a long life, full of blessing. *Ephesians 6:1-3*

Footprint Jesus was obedient to his parents. And as he grew taller he grew wiser, and was loved by God and man. *Luke 2:51-52 Story 148*

186

A PROMISE FOR YOUR PARENTS

If parents bring up their children with the loving discipline the Lord himself approves, with suggestions and godly advice, teaching them to choose the right path, then when they are older, they will remain on it. *Proverbs 22:6 Ephesians 6:4*

Footprint It is a wonderful heritage to have honest and godly parents. Thank God for your parents and all they've taught you. *Proverbs 14:26 / 20:7*

TEN COMMANDMENTS FOR KIDS

1. Thou shalt not have any other parents but your own. (What your friends say, the way other people do it, and what they do on TV don't count.)
2. Thou shalt not bow down and worship the TV, video games, the computer, or anything else. (Some time must be spent relating with people.)
3. Thou shalt accept cheaper products and not take their names in vain. (Name brands aren't always necessary.)
4. Remember weekend mornings and keep them quiet. (Running and yelling, making messes, fighting, inviting all the neighbors in, and loud music are not allowed.)
5. Honor your father and mother. (This means obey, love, cuddle, hug, kiss, and think the world of your parents— and always eat your vegetables!)
6. Thou shalt not attempt to kill, fight, or argue with your brothers and sisters. (Remember: anyone who looks like you can't be all bad.)
7. Thou shalt not commit parental adultery. (Don't ask someone else's parents to adopt you because they're always so nice to you; their kids probably wish your parents would adopt them.)
8. Thou shalt not steal. (This includes sneaking cookies, borrowing things without asking, and playing with Dad's toys when he's not around.)
9. Thou shalt not tell lies. (Remember: truth is like a lump of modeling clay. You can bend and stretch it and shape it into something else, but your parents can always find out what it really looks like by applying pressure. So tell the truth to start with.)
10. Thou shalt not covet. (This means don't even ask for things you see advertised on TV.)

PART TWENTY-ONE

FAME, FAVOR, AND HONOR

PROMOTION COMES FROM GOD

Next Assignment

God decides who will get awards and honors. So patiently trust him to put you where he wants you to be, and in his good time he will lift you up. *Psalm 75:6-7 1 Peter 5:6*

Footprint The disciples were arguing about which one of them would be the greatest in Jesus' kingdom. Do you remember what Jesus said? *Luke 22:24-27 Story 172*

GOD WILL HONOR YOU

When you follow Jesus, the Father will honor you. He will prize and respect you and cause others to as well.
Proverbs 22:4 John 12:26

Footprint   God's idea of a hero is different than the world's. Having God think highly of you and your actions is all that really matters. What kind of person is a hero in God's eyes? *Romans 12:9-21 Psalms 1:1-3 / 15*

A Good Reputation

A good reputation is more valuable than the most expensive perfume. So live a peaceful life, mind your own business, and do your work. Then people who are not Christians will trust and respect you. *Ecclesiastes 7:1 1 Thessalonians 4:11-12*

Footprint   The Lord helped David do everything well, and all the people loved him! *1 Samuel 18:28-30 Story 81*

GOD WILL GIVE YOU FAVOR

38 FAVORS

If you want favor with both God and man and a reputation for good judgment and common sense, then trust the Lord completely; don't ever trust your own way. In everything you do, put God first, and he will direct you and make your efforts successful. *Proverbs 3:4-6*

Footprint When Daniel and his friends first went to Babylon, they did some pretty strange things in the eyes of the Babylonians. But Daniel and his friends weren't worried about the Babylonians, they wanted to please God. Read *Daniel 2:48-49 / 10:11* and *Story 131* to see if these men won favor with God or man or both.

193

FAVOR, FAME, HONOR

Favor is:
- when people trust you without always having to check up on what you're doing
- being asked to do an important job because you have faithfully done a small job well
- when your family makes your birthday an extra special occasion

Fame is:
- when people you've never met before respect you because of your good reputation
- being the kind of person that people are happy to have around
- when everyone in school knows who you are because you tell them about God and always do what is right

Honor is:
- when others think enough of you to ask your advice
- when people recognize and thank you for a job well done
- when your friends and family tell you how proud they are of you

When you become a child of God, you have favor, fame, and honor in his eyes—always! And what God thinks about you is more important than what anyone else says.

PART TWENTY-TWO

TELLING OTHERS ABOUT JESUS

GOD WILL HELP YOU
TELL OTHERS ABOUT JESUS

If anybody asks why you believe in God's way, be ready to tell them. The Holy Spirit will help you and give you the right words to speak. With him helping you, you won't be afraid to tell others about Jesus. *Acts 1:8 2 Timothy 1:8 1 Peter 3:15*

Footprint   When the disciples were told that they would be punished if they preached about Jesus, they prayed and asked God to help them not be afraid, then they went out and preached anyway. Sometimes it is downright scary telling people about God. Ask him to give you courage. *Acts 4:24-31 Story 180*

196

GOD WILL CONFIRM WHAT YOU SAY ABOUT JESUS

After Jesus returned to heaven, Christians told the good news of Jesus everywhere. And the Lord was with them and confirmed what they said by the miracles that followed their message. *Mark 16:20*

Footprint   When Paul heard God speaking to him and accepted Christ, his whole life was transformed. Even his name was changed! But many of the Christians were still afraid that Paul wanted to persecute them. But God gave Paul the ability to preach and teach so that others would believe what he said about Christ. *Acts 9:26-28*

YOU CAN DO GREATER WORKS

Jesus said, "In solemn truth I tell you, anyone believing in me shall do the same miracles I have done, and even greater ones. You can ask him for anything using my name, and I will do it, for this will bring praise to the Father." *John 14:12-13*

Footprint   Don't be afraid to trust God for great miracles. Read *Stories 101, 107 and 108, 1 Kings 16–17 and 2 Kings 3–4.* God is quite experienced when it comes to miracles.

GOD WILL BLESS YOU WHEN OTHERS MAKE FUN OF YOU FOR BEING A CHRISTIAN

Jesus said, "Happy are those who are persecuted because they are good, for the Kingdom of Heaven is theirs. When you are made fun of and persecuted and lied about because you are my followers—wonderful! Be happy about it! Be very glad! For a tremendous reward awaits you up in heaven." *Matthew 5:10-12*

Footprint If you are kind when people make fun of you because of your faith, you are acting like Jesus would act, and he will help you. *Acts 7:54-60 Story 181*

PRAYER OF SALVATION

Pray and believe this prayer, and Jesus will forgive you and come into your life. Then tell others about Jesus and let them pray this as well.

Father God, the Bible says that everyone has sinned, and the punishment for sin is death. But it also says that you sent your son Jesus to take the punishment for everyone's sins by dying for them and rising again from the dead, so that those who ask you to forgive them can live forever.

So please forgive me of my sins and give me eternal life. I know that Jesus died for me. I trust you now to save me from the consequences of my sin. I owe you my life, and I give it to you now to use for your work.

Please teach me and help me live the way you want me to. And show me your plan for my future. Thank you for making me your child.

In Jesus' name. Amen.

PART TWENTY-THREE

YOU AND OTHERS

GOD WILL BLESS THOSE WHO BLESS YOU

When you are following God's plan for your life, you will be a blessing to many people. So God will also bless anyone who helps you because they see that you are his child and are helping others. *Genesis 12:2-3 Galatians 3:8-9*

Footprint   God blessed Potiphar just because Joseph, God's servant, was in his home! *Genesis 39:1-6 Story 20*

GOD WILL HELP YOU GET ALONG WITH OTHERS

God will help you live in complete harmony with those around you. So be kind to others, tenderhearted and forgiving just as God has forgiven you because you belong to Christ.
Romans 15:5 Ephesians 4:32

Footprint   Great things happen when you get together with other people and cooperate. In *Story 42 Exodus 35-40* God provides people with different materials and different skills. It is only when they come together that great things happen.

203

GOD WILL HELP YOU STAND UP TO PEER PRESSURE

When your friends try to get you to do something wrong, the Lord will rescue you and help you to escape. But it's best to avoid trouble and not hang around with people like that. Instead, enjoy the friendship of those who love the Lord and have a pure heart.

Psalm 1:1-2 1 Corinthians 10:13 2 Timothy 2:22 2 Peter 2:9

Footprint   Remember Balaam? He should have never even considered Balak's offer, but he let peer pressure get the best of him. Ask God to help you stand up to peer pressure. *Numbers 22 Story 52*

THE GOLDEN RULE

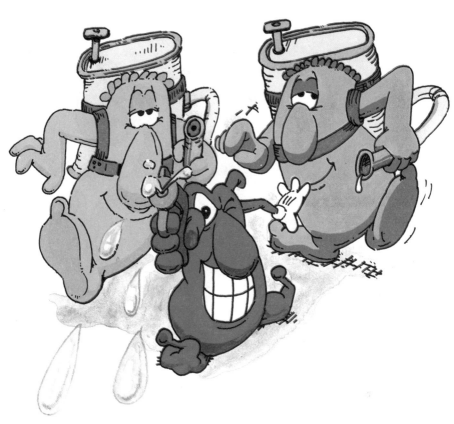

How you treat others is how they will treat you. If you are nice to others, people will be nice to you. But if you are mean to others, people will be mean to you.
Proverbs 11:24-25 / 26:27 Luke 6:31

Footprint Read what happened to the people who tricked the King into throwing Daniel into the lions' den. What do you think God thought of how they treated Daniel?
Daniel 6:24 Story 135

GOD WILL HELP YOU LOVE OTHERS

God is love! When you love him and others, you are living with God and God is living in you, and he will cause your love to grow more perfect and complete. *1 John 4:16-17, 20-21*

Footprint   "If anyone says, 'I love God,' but keeps on hating his brother, he is a liar; for if he doesn't love his brother who is right there in front of him, how can he love God whom he has never seen?" Is there someone you have a hard time loving? Ask God for his help. *1 John 4:20*

GOD WILL GIVE YOU PEACE WITH YOUR ENEMIES

When you are trying to please God, he will make even your worst enemies to be at peace with you. *Proverbs 16:7*

Footprint If your enemy is thirsty give him something to drink, then he will feel ashamed of himself for what he did to you. *Romans 12:20*

TRUE LOVE

Love is very patient and kind,
never jealous or envious,
never boastful or proud,
never haughty or selfish or rude.

Love does not demand its own way.

It is not irritable or touchy.

It does not hold grudges
and will hardly even notice
when others do it wrong.

It is never glad about injustice,
but rejoices whenever truth wins out.

If you love someone you will be loyal to him
no matter what the cost.

You will always believe in him,
always expect the best of him,
and always stand your ground in defending him.

There are three things that remain—
faith, hope and love—
and the greatest of these is love.
1 Corinthians 13

208

PART TWENTY-FOUR

YOU CAN DO IT

YOU DON'T HAVE TO QUIT

Don't get tired of doing what is right, for after a while you will reap a harvest of blessing if you don't get discouraged and give up. *Galatians 6:9*

Footprint Nehemiah took on a tough job—he decided to rebuild the wall around Jerusalem. It was a complicated job, and two evil men tried to distract him. But Nehemiah was a determined man, and God blessed his efforts. Read about Nehemiah's job and the celebration they had when it was completed. *Stories 143–144*

GOD WILL ENCOURAGE YOU

He wonderfully comforts and strengthens you in your hardships and trials. And why does he do this? So that when others are troubled, needing your sympathy and encouragement, you can pass on to them this same help and comfort God has given you. *2 Corinthians 1:3-5*

Footprint   *Isaiah 40:27-31* is a special promise to remember when you feel discouraged. Memorize it so that you can share it with someone who needs encouragement.

GOD WILL GIVE YOU THE ABILITY TO DO HIS WILL

GOD'S HAND

kid's clay

When God wants you to do something, he will give you his power and a special ability to do it well. He will make sure you are well prepared and fully equipped.

Ephesians 3:7 2 Timothy 3:17 Hebrews 13:21

Footprint Before Jesus went back to heaven, he gave his disciples an assignment, but he also told them to wait for something to happen before beginning their work. Read *Acts 1:4-8* and *Story 179* and find out what the disciples were waiting for. In the same way God always enables us to do the job he assigns us.

GOD WILL GIVE YOU THE STRENGTH TO DO HIS WILL

You can do everything God asks you to with the help of Christ who gives you the strength and power. *Philippians 4:13*

Footprint   God gave Noah a big job—one that took over one hundred years to complete. God also gave Noah the strength to do that job. God will not ask you to do something for him and then take his hands away from your life. He is always in touch with you—strengthening you and encouraging you. *Genesis 6–8 Story 4*

GOD WILL STRENGTHEN YOU WITH PATIENCE

Is your life full of difficulties and temptations? Then be happy, for when the way is rough, your patience has a chance to grow. So let it grow, and don't try to squirm out of your problems. For when your patience is finally in full bloom, then you will be ready for anything, strong in character, full and complete. *James 1:2-4 Galatians 5:22*

Footprint   Follow the example of those who receive all that God has promised them because of their strong faith and patience. *Hebrews 6:12*

GOD HAS GIVEN YOU EVERYTHING YOU NEED FOR DOING HIS WILL

God will equip you with all you need for doing his will. And he will produce in you all that is pleasing to him through the power of Christ. *Hebrews 13:20-21*

Footprint   When God told Moses to lead the people out of Egypt, Moses said that he wasn't equipped for the job. Do you remember what God told him? *Exodus 2–4 Story 29*

GOD WILL STRENGTHEN YOU WITH SELF-CONTROL

The Holy Spirit will help you be self-controlled. And as you learn to control yourself and put aside your own desires, you will become patient and wise, gladly letting God have his way with you. *Galatians 5:22 2 Peter 1:6*

Footprint   Some areas that are important to practice self-control in are your temper, your diet, your body, your speech and your own desires. *Proverbs 16:32 1 Corinthians 9:27 / 6:12-13 James 3:2 2 Peter 1:6*

STAY STRONG AND STEADY AND YOU WILL FINISH THE RACE

Since future victory is sure, be strong and steady, always doing what the Lord wants you to do. Forget the past and look forward to what lies ahead. Strain to reach the end of the race. For then you will finally be all that Christ wants you to be, and you will receive the prize for which God is calling you up to heaven. *1 Corinthians 15:58 Philippians 3:12-14*

Footprint   Paul's life was full of persecution and suffering because he faithfully obeyed God even when it wasn't the easy thing to do. Read what Paul says about his life in *2 Timothy 4:6-8.* Paul knew that he had run a good race and was looking forward to his reward.

DON'T GIVE UP

Here are five things to do whenever you feel like giving up.

1. PRAY—Ask God for comfort. The Holy Spirit is called the Comforter; he'll help you feel better so that you can keep on going. *John 14:15-16 2 Corinthians 1:3-5*

2. CHECK—Did you put God first and find out if the thing you are doing is what he wanted? If the answer is yes, then be confident that everything will work out. If no, ask God for his wisdom and direction right now before going any further. *Proverbs 3:6 James 1:5-6 / 4:13-16*

3. TRUST—Stop worrying! If you've prayed about your situation, then start thanking God for his answers. Then his peace will keep your thoughts and your heart quiet and at rest as you trust in him. *Philippians 4:6-7 2 Peter 5:7*

4. STAND—Keep your eyes focused on the truth. Don't let go of what you're trusting God for. And don't give up! STAND FIRM! *Ephesians 6:13 2 Thessalonians 2:15*

5. REMEMBER—God has promised that if you don't get tired and give up, you will reap a harvest of blessing. And everything will work out for you in the best way possible. *Romans 8:28 Galatians 6:9*

PART TWENTY-FIVE
LEADERS

GOD WILL HELP YOUR LEADERS WHEN YOU PRAY FOR THEM

Pray for God's mercy upon the rulers of your country and all others who are in authority over you. For when God is helping these people, you will be able to live in peace and quietness, because your leaders will be making godly decisions. *1 Timothy 2:1-3*

Footprint God provided just the right leader for the Jews when an evil person tried to destroy them. Read *Esther* and *Stories 139–142* to learn more about this special leader. Then ask God to help your leaders make wise decisions.

GOD HAS GIVEN YOU SPIRITUAL LEADERS TO WATCH OVER YOU

Obey your spiritual leaders, for God has put them in charge of you. Give them reason to report joyfully about you to the Lord and not with sorrow. *Hebrews 13:17*

Footprint   Remember the people who have taught you the Word of God. Think of all the good in them, and try to trust the Lord as they do. *Hebrews 13:7 Story 106*

221

GOD WILL GIVE YOU GOOD LEADERS

God will appoint responsible leaders to care for you; leaders who will lead and teach you willingly and who are eager to serve the Lord, leaders after his own heart, who will lead you by their good example and guide you with wisdom and understanding. *Jeremiah 3:15 / 23:4 1 Peter 5:1-4*

Footprint The people of Israel needed good leaders. When they allowed God to choose their leaders, he provided great men and women to do the job. *Stories 63–65* tell about some of the leaders God selected. Notice what the Israelis did when they didn't have a good leader. Thank God for the leaders he has given you.

GOD WILL HELP YOU LEAD OTHERS

If you are given the responsibility of leading others, trust God to help you. Then God's wisdom and power will help you in all that you do. He will even direct your thoughts and guide your decisions.

Proverbs 1:5-6 / 16:10 / 21:1 1 Corinthians 6:4-7

Footprint   Solomon used God's wisdom to lead. Once two women both claimed to be the mother of a baby. Read how Solomon used wisdom to find out who was telling the truth. *1 Kings 3:17-28*

GOD SPEAKS ABOUT GOVERNMENT

Obey the government, for God is the one who has put it there. There is no government anywhere that God has not placed in power. People who refuse to obey the laws of the land are refusing to obey God, and punishment will follow. The policeman does not frighten people who are doing right, but those doing evil will always fear him. So if you don't want to be afraid, keep the law and you will get along well. The policeman is sent by God to help you. But if you are doing something wrong, of course you should be afraid, for he will have you punished. He is sent by God for that very purpose. Obey the laws, then, for two reasons: first, to keep from being punished, and second, just because you know you should.

Pay your taxes also, for these same two reasons. For government workers need to be paid so that they can keep on doing God's work, serving you. Pay everyone whatever he ought to have; pay your taxes and import duties gladly, obey those over you, and give honor and respect to all those to whom it is due. *Romans 13:1-7*

PART TWENTY-SIX
SUCCESS

PROSPERITY IS A GIFT FROM GOD

Do you delight in doing everything God wants you to? Are you always thinking about him and ways to follow him more closely? If so, then you are like a tree on a river bank, that always has luscious fruit. God will bless your life and cause it to prosper. *Psalm 1:1-3*

Footprint   Read about King Hezekiah. God prospered him in everything he did. Then when God prospers you remember that God did it, not you. *2 Kings 18:6-7 Story 123*

THE PRINCIPLES OF SUCCESS

When you follow God's principles, you will receive his rewards. To have a successful life: ● Love wisdom. ● Trust God for success. ● Commit your work to the Lord. ● Admit your mistakes and change. ● Listen to advice. ● Be kind and good to others. ● Obey God's word. ● Work hard.
Psalm 37:3 Proverbs 12:3, 24 / 13:13 / 15:22 / 16:3, 11 / 19:8 / 21:5 / 28:13, 25

Footprint Climbing God's ladder of success may be tough going sometimes, but it's worth it because God will reward your efforts.

227

WEALTH AND RICHES

Wealth and riches are gifts from God. But don't trust in money which will soon be gone. You are rich because God owns everything. As you trust him he will always give you all that you need and more.
Deuteronomy 8:18 Matthew 6:19-20 Philippians 4:19 2 Timothy 6:17

Footprint   Jesus told a parable about a rich fool who stored up treasures here on earth instead of in heaven. Read *Story 156 Luke 12:15-21* to find out what happened to this man.

GOD WILL GIVE YOU TRUE RICHES

Shadows of Truth

Some "rich" people are poor, and some "poor" people have great wealth. Do you want to be truly rich? You already are if you are happy and good. For the true riches of heaven and the Lord's blessing are your greatest wealth and they can't be bought with money. *Proverbs 10:22 / 13:7 Luke 16:11 1 Timothy 6:6-8*

Footprint May the Lord continually bless you with heaven's blessings as well as with human joys. *Psalm 128:5*

229

JESUS SAID

Don't store up treasures here on earth where they can rust away or be stolen. Store them in heaven where they will never lose their value and are safe from thieves. If your treasures are in heaven, your heart will be there too.

You cannot serve two masters—God and money. For you will hate one and love the other, or the other way around.

So my counsel is: Don't worry about things—food, drink and clothes. Look at the birds! They don't worry about what to eat—they don't need to sow or reap or store up food—for your heavenly Father feeds them. And you are far more valuable to him than they are. Will all your worries add a single moment to your life?

And why worry about clothes? Look at the field of lilies! They don't worry about theirs. Yet King Solomon in all his glory was not clothed as beautifully as they. And if God cares so wonderfully for flowers that are here today and gone tomorrow, won't he more surely care for you!

So don't worry at all about having enough food and clothing. Why be like non-Christians? For they take pride in all these things and are deeply concerned about them. But your heavenly Father already knows perfectly well that you need them, and he will give them to you if you give him first place in your life and live as he wants you to. *Matthew 6:19-20, 24-33*

GOD IS YOUR CONFIDENCE

BOLDNESS

God will give you the boldness to stand up for what you
believe in no matter what anyone else may think, say or do.
And that boldness will be a clear sign from God, that he is
with you. The wicked run away when no one is even chasing
them! But the godly are as bold as lions!
Proverbs 28:1 Philippians 1:27-28 Hebrews 13:5-6

Footprint   When the Jewish leaders realized that Peter
and John were uneducated fishermen, and yet were so bold,
they were amazed. Their boldness came from God, and
yours does too. *Acts 4:13 Story 179*

COURAGE

God will never fail you nor forsake you. That is why you can be strong and courageous. For when the Lord is your helper how can you be afraid of anything?
Deuteronomy 31:6 1 Chronicles 22:13 Hebrews 13:5-6

Footprint   Do you know who had so much courage because God was on his side that he was willing to take on a whole army with only one other man to help him? *1 Samuel 14:1-23 Story 78*

233

FAITH

Faith is the tool that God has given you to beat sin and evil and to be able to do everything he asks you to do. Trials and problems test your faith to see if it is strong and pure because your faith is very precious to God. If it remains strong after being tested in the test tube of fiery trials, it will bring you honor on the day of Christ's return.

Romans 12:3 1 Peter 1:7 1 John 5:3-4

Footprint Read *James 1:12* and make your own sword and crown. Use the sword to remind you that faith is the problem solver, and wear the crown to remind you of the reward God has promised you if your faith is strong.

TRUST

Those who trust in the Lord are as steady as a mountain, unmoved by any circumstance. *Psalm 125:1*

Footprint   Here's another promise to encourage you when trouble comes. "Because you love me, I will rescue you; I will make you great because you trust in my name. When you call on me I will answer; I will be with you in trouble, and rescue you and honor you. I will satisfy you with a full life and give you my salvation." *Psalm 91:14-16*

FAMOUS FIGURES OF FAITH

What is faith? It is the confident assurance that something we hope for is going to happen. It is the certainty that what we hope for is waiting for us, even though we cannot see it up ahead. Men of God in the Bible were famous for their faith.

Enoch had faith in God, and that is why God took him away to heaven without dying; suddenly he was gone because God took him. Before this happened, God had said how pleased he was with Enoch. You can never please God without faith, without depending on him.

Noah was another person who trusted God. When he heard God's warning about the future, Noah believed God even though there was no sign of a flood. And wasting no time, he built the ark and saved his family. And because of his faith he became one of those whom God accepted.

Abraham trusted God, and when God told him to leave home and go far away to another land which he promised to give him, Abraham obeyed. Away he went, not even knowing where he was going.

Sarah had faith, too, and because of this she was able to become a mother in spite of her old age. She realized that God, who gave her his promise, would certainly do what he said. And so a whole nation came from Abraham and Sarah, who were too old to have even one child.

All of these people were glad to do whatever God wanted them to because they knew that this earth was not their real home. They understood that they were just strangers visiting down here. They were living for heaven. And now God is not ashamed to be called their God. *Hebrews 11*

236

HEALTH

HEALTHY BODIES ARE A GIFT FROM GOD

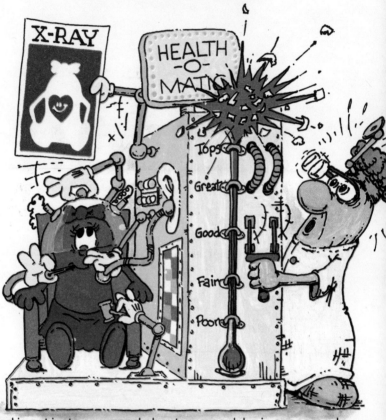

God is not just concerned about your soul; he is concerned about the health of your body too. Paul said that our bodies are the "temple" where God lives now. He said we should stay away from things that hurt us and keep our temple strong and clean. *1 Corinthians 3:16, 17 2 Corinthians 6:16*

Footprint   Do you have a healthy body? Good health is a wonderful gift from God. Many people are not healthy, and they may never be able to see, hear, or even walk. Have you thanked God today for your healthy body? *Psalms 92:1-5 / 139:14 Story 35*

238

GOD HAS THE POWER TO HEAL YOUR BODY

If you get sick, call for the elders of the church and have them pray for you and pour a little oil on you, asking the Lord to heal you. And their prayer, if offered in faith, and if part of God's plan, will heal you, for the Lord has the power to make you well. *James 5:14-15*

Footprint   Who do you go to for help when you feel sick? God has given us parents and doctors to help us get better. But we can go directly to God in prayer because he made our bodies. One of the names that God calls himself is "The Lord That Heals You." *Exodus 15:26*

GOD HAS THE POWER TO PROTECT YOU FROM SICKNESS

Sickness sometimes tests our love for God, but nevertheless, God has the power to shelter you so that it can't come near. *Exodus 15:26 Psalms 91:9-10 / 119:67-71*

Footprint Sickness entered the world because of sin, but Jesus already bore all of the penalties of your sins. When Jesus comes back, all sin, sickness, and death will be gone forever. *Isaiah 53:4-5 1 Peter 2:24-25 Revelation 21:4 Story 175*

240

PHYSICAL STRENGTH AND ENERGY COME FROM GOD

When you trust and reverence the Lord, he can give you renewed health and vitality. And as you learn wisdom, storing up God's words in your heart, you will be filled with living energy and inner strength. *Proverbs 3:7-8 / 4:20-22 Daniel 1:8-21*

Footprint They that wait upon the Lord shall renew their strength. They shall mount up with wings like eagles; they shall run and not be weary; they shall walk and not faint. *Isaiah 40:31*

THE SNAKE ON A POLE

The Israelis got very tired of traveling through the wilderness and sinned by rebelling against God and their leader, Moses. "We have no bread and no water, and we hate this manna!" they complained.

The Lord was angry and sent serpents into the camp to bite the people, causing many of them to die.

They ran to Moses, screaming, "We have sinned, for we have complained against the Lord and against you. Please pray that the serpents will go away."

So Moses prayed for them. The Lord told Moses to make a bronze snake that would look like the poisonous snakes that were biting the people.

"Put the bronze snake on a pole," God said. "Whenever anyone is bitten, if he just looks at the snake on the pole, he will get well again."

So Moses made the bronze snake and put it on the top of a pole. Many people looked at it and lived instead of dying from their snakebites.

The snake on the pole is just like Jesus, who took our sins on himself and was hung on a cross. And just as the Israelis didn't die but recovered from the snakebites when they looked at the snake on the pole, when you trust in Jesus you are saved from the bite of sin. On the cross, Jesus conquered sin along with death and disease, and when he comes back he will wipe them out forever.

Numbers 21:4-9 Deuteronomy 28:15-19, 58-61 John 3:14-15 Galatians 3:13 Revelation 21:4

PART TWENTY-NINE

PROVISION

GOD WILL PROVIDE EVERYTHING YOU NEED

Don't worry about anything; instead, pray about everything; tell God your needs and don't forget to thank him for his answers. For he will give you everything you need and more from his riches in heaven, because you are his child. *2 Corinthians 9:8 Philippians 4:6, 19*

Footprint   God knows exactly what you need even before you ask him! He even knows the number of hairs on your head. So trust him to provide for you and thank him for everything he does. *Matthew 6:7-8 Luke 12:7 Story 159*

244

GOD IS ON TIME
WHEN WE NEED HIS HELP

If you go boldly to the very throne of God and stay there, you will receive his mercy and find grace to help you in your time of need. *Hebrews 4:16*

Footprint   God is on time, but sometimes what we think is the right time, really isn't. God has promised you that everything that happens to you is working out for your good. *Romans 8:28*

GOD WILL WORK OUT EVERY DETAIL IN YOUR LIFE

God made you, and he knows everything about you, even the smallest details of your life. So if you love God and desire to follow him, you can be sure that everything that happens to you will work out for your good. *Psalm 138:8 / 139:1-3 Romans 8:28*

Footprint   To see how God wonderfully works out every detail, read the story of Ruth. *Story 71*

GOD WILL PROVIDE YOUR FOOD

God will give you the food you need each day. For example, look at the birds! They don't worry about what to eat—they don't have a farm or buy a lot of food to store up—for your heavenly Father feeds them. And you are far more valuable to him than they are! *Matthew 6:11, 26*

Footprint   God provides what you need each day, so don't worry about tomorrow. Read about how God used four lepers to feed a whole city. *2 Kings 7 Story 110*

GOD WILL BLESS YOUR FOOD

Every kind of food that God made is good, and you may eat it gladly if you are thankful for it and if you ask God to bless it.
1 Timothy 4:4-5

Footprint Here are some examples of people blessing their food: Samuel—*1 Samuel 9:13*, Jesus—*Matthew 14:19*, Paul—*Acts 27:35*.

248

GOD WILL PROVIDE YOU WITH CLOTHING

Look at the flowers! They never have to worry about clothes. Yet King Solomon in all his glory was not clothed as beautifully as they are. And if God cares so wonderfully for flowers that are here today and gone tomorrow, he will surely care for you and provide you with clothing. *Matthew 6:28-30*

Footprint   God promises to take care of all our needs, so don't worry about what you will wear. And remember, God wants our beauty to come from inside us, not just from what we put on our bodies. *1 Peter 3:3-4*

THANKFUL FOR

Lord, I'm thankful for:

Big and small,
   first and last.
Here's some things,
   I'll say them fast.

Watermelon, popcorn,
   hot dogs, and ice-cream cones.
Basketball, baseball,
   football, and skipping stones.

Hide and seek, tag ("You're it!"),
   hopscotch, and skipping rope,
Holding hands, bro and sis,
   good friends, and telling jokes.

Camping trips, holidays,
   sunshine, and swimming pools.
Christmas time, Easter eggs,
   birthdays, and April fools.

Singing songs, laughing hard,
   music loud, and making noise.
Television, cartoons,
   videos, and brand new toys.

Mom and Dad, family time,
   reading books, and shadow lights
Comfy bed, sleepy eyes,
   hugging close, and long good nights.

PART THIRTY
A GOOD LIFE

A Truly Good Life

Learn to know God better and better. For as you know him better, he will give you, through his great power, everything you need for living a truly good life. *2 Peter 1:2-3*

Footprint   Peter tells us some of the things we need to learn in order to have a truly good life that pleases God. Read *1 Peter 1:2-9* and make a list of these things.

GOD WILL FILL YOUR LIFE WITH JOY

It is great to receive good things from the Lord and to have the health to enjoy them. For to enjoy your work and to accept willingly God's plan for your life is indeed a gift from God. When you do these things you will not need to look back with sorrow on your past, for God will have given you joy.
Ecclesiastes 5:20

Footprint   The prophet Isaiah tells us to have confidence in God's plans because they are always better than our own. Read *Isaiah 55:8-13* to discover the goodness of God when we trust him and do his will.

AN EXCITING LIFE

Thank you Lord!

Jesus' purpose is to give you a full and good life. Yes, God wants you to experience good things and to have an exciting life that you can love and enjoy.
Psalm 16:11 Proverbs 2:20-21 / 14:14 John 10:10

Footprint Even though God makes life enjoyable, he does not want you to spend all of your time running after the pleasures of this life; for that can draw you away from God. Gehazi fell into this trap. Read and find out what happened to him. *2 Kings 5 Proverbs 21:17 Luke 8:14 Story 156*

HAPPINESS

Life is not always easy, but if you try to serve God before trying to get things for yourself, God will be with you and will give you true happiness. The greatest happiness always comes from serving and reverencing God and from helping others. *Psalm 128:1-2 Matthew 6:33*

Footprint   What is the best way to find happiness and receive God's blessing? Read the Beatitudes in *Matthew 5:3-12* and see what kinds of people are blessed with true happiness. Are you one of these blessed and happy people?

GOD WILL BE WITH YOU IN DIFFICULTIES

Your life may contain struggles and difficulties, but these are your opportunities to know God's strength to help you. God goes with you and gives you joy and patience even in the hard times. Stay on God's path and you'll get to know just how delightful it really is.
Psalm 119:35 Proverbs 15:19 Isaiah 26:7 James 1

Footprint If something blocks your pathway in life and starts to make it difficult, don't complain like the Israelis did at the Red Sea. Trust God! He'll take care of the sea and the Egyptians in your life. *Exodus 14 Story 35*

Long Life Is a Gift from God

God knows exactly how long every person will live. A long and full life is a gift from God. The most important thing is for you to try to please God every day. Then whether your life is short or long, you know you have lived the best life possible.
Job 5:26 Psalm 91:16

Footprint   How old are you? Who is the oldest person you know? *Genesis 5:27* says that Methuselah lived for 969 years. If you obey and believe in God, you will probably live a long life, but better yet, you will live longer than Methuselah— you will live forever!

257

GOD WILL GIVE YOU PEACE

Jesus said, "I am leaving you with a gift — peace of mind and heart! And the peace I give isn't fragile like the peace the world gives. So don't be troubled or afraid." Even when life around you is not peaceful, you can have inner peace because you know Jesus.

Proverbs 1:33 Isaiah 28:12 John 14:27 1 Timothy 2:2

Footprint   Which would you rather eat: a dry crust of bread or a juicy steak? *Proverbs 17:1* says that a dry crust eaten in peace is better than steak every day along with argument and strife. Try to get along well with everyone. You'll make life better for them—and better for yourself as well!

258

MORE TIME

Reverence for God adds hours to each day; and using God's wisdom will make your day more profitable and the years of your life more fruitful. *Proverbs 9:11 / 10:27*

Footprint Read about the unusual way God provided more time for Joshua when he was in a sticky situation. *Joshua 10:12-15 Story 60*

SEARCHING FOR THE GOOD LIFE

Get a piece of paper and write down all the "good life" words you can find.

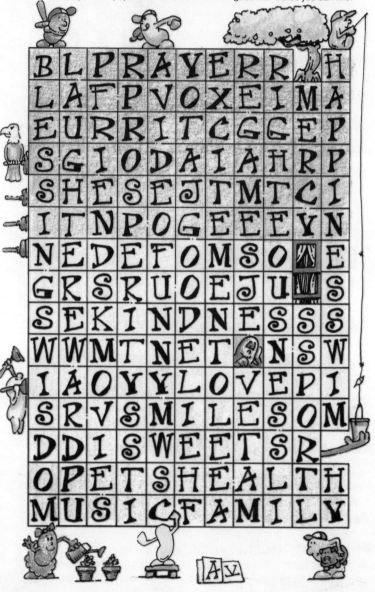

```
B L P R A Y E R R   H
L A F P V O X E I M A
E U R R I T C G G E P
S G I O D A I A H R P
S H E S E J T M T C I
I T N P O G E E E Y N
N E D E F O M S O   E
G R S R U O E J U   S
S E K I N D N E S S S
W W M T N E T   N S W
I A O Y Y L O V E P I
S R V S M I L E S O M
D D I S W E E T S R
O P E T S H E A L T H
M U S I C F A M I L Y
```

260

PART THIRTY-ONE

HELPING OTHERS

GOD GIVES TO YOU SO YOU CAN GIVE TO OTHERS

God loves it when you give cheerfully. He rewards you by giving you everything you need, and more. Yes, God gives you so much so that you can give away much.
2 Corinthians 9:7-11

Footprint   Cheerful givers are always willing to give, even when they have very little. Read about the poor widow who gave more than the rich people. Have you ever given away as much as she did? She gave everything she had.
Matthew 12:41-44

GOD GIVES TO YOU IN THE SAME WAY YOU GIVE TO OTHERS

When you give much away to others, your gifts will often return to you in full and overflowing measure. Although you should not give just to get something back, whatever measure you use to give—large or small—will be used to measure what is given back to you when Jesus comes back with his reward. *Luke 6:38*

Footprint   It is possible to give away everything you own and become richer! It is also possible to hold on to your belongings too tightly and lose everything. What advice did Jesus have for a rich man who held on to his money too tightly? *Luke 18:22 Proverbs 11:24-25*

GOD WILL REWARD YOU FOR HELPING THE POOR

When you help the poor you are lending to the Lord. We are told never to turn away a stranger or poor person in need of help. That person might even be an angel in disguise! Our service to the poor is service to God, so learn to be generous. *Proverbs 19:17 / 28:27 Hebrews 13:2*

Footprint   Jesus said that when you give to the poor you are really giving to him. Don't leave Jesus hungry or out in the cold. Keep a look out for poor people who you can help with food or clothing. *Matthew 25:31-46 Story 171*

GOD WILL REWARD YOU FOR GIVING TO HIS WORK

You cannot take riches with you when you die. Instead of storing up wealth, honor the Lord by giving him part of all your income. For when you give to God's work, you store up riches in heaven that will never disappear.
Proverbs 3:9-10 Matthew 6:19-21 Philippians 4:15-17, 19

Footprint If you give to God's work consistently and generously, he will open up the windows of heaven and pour out a blessing so great you won't have room enough to take it in. *Malachi 3:10*

WHEN YOU SHARE YOU WILL ALWAYS HAVE ENOUGH

When you have plenty, you should divide what you have with those who are in need. God will make sure that what you have left will always be enough. *2 Corinthians 8:13-15*

Footprint John said, "If you have two coats, give one to the poor. If you have extra food, give it away to those who are hungry." Read about John the Baptist in *Luke 3* and *Story 148*.

GOD WILL MAKE YOU A WALKING BLESSING

When you listen to God's voice, obey him, and believe his promises, you will be a blessing to other people. You will be their example, a pattern for them to follow—someone who shows them what it means to live with love, faith, and clean thoughts. *Genesis 12:1-3 Galatians 3:8-9 1 Timothy 4:12*

Footprint   Jesus was a blessing wherever he went, and he is your example. Do you bring joy and blessing to all the people around you? Do people miss you when you're not there to help? *John 13:15 / 21:25*

267

GOD WILL USE YOU TO GET HIS HELP TO OTHERS

God wants you to bring others to Jesus and has made you his messenger. He will work in you so that you can teach people about God and his ways.
2 Corinthians 5:18-20 Hebrews 1:1-2

Footprint   Jesus said, "If anyone is thirsty let him come to me and drink." Once you believe, others can drink from the river of living water in you. *John 7:37-38*

THE PROMISE OF GREATNESS

Jesus said, "Anyone wanting to be the greatest must be the servant of all. The more lowly your service to others, the greater you are!" *Matthew 23:11 Mark 9:35*

Footprint   Only slaves washed people's feet in Bible times. Yet Jesus gladly washed his disciples' feet. Can you think of some ways to serve other people? *John 13 Story 172*

THE GOOD SAMARITAN

The Bible says to love God and your neighbors. Once a lawyer asked Jesus, "Who is my neighbor?"

Jesus answered by telling him this story: "A man was traveling from Jerusalem to Jericho, but some robbers stopped him, stole his clothing, and beat him up. He was seriously wounded, and the robbers left him half dead beside the road. While he lay there on the ground, too weak to get up, a Jewish priest went by. He was a minister and a teacher of God's law, but instead of being kind to the wounded man, he crossed over to the other side of the road and went on, pretending he didn't see the man lying there. Next, a Levite came along (Levites were the men who helped people worship at the temple), but when he saw the man, he too went right on without trying to help him.

"But then a Samaritan came by. The Jews and the Samaritans hated each other, so it wouldn't have been surprising if this Samaritan had refused to help the wounded Jew. But when he saw him, he pitied him, pulled out his first-aid kit, and bandaged up his wounds and put medicine on them. Then he helped him onto the back of his donkey and took him to an inn and paid the man's bill.

"Which of these three was a neighbor to the wounded man?" Jesus asked the lawyer.

"The one who helped him," the lawyer replied.

Then Jesus told him, "Go and do the same to everyone who needs your help."

Jesus meant that people who say they love God must prove it by being kind to others. *Luke 10:25-37 Story 163*

PART THIRTY-TWO
DIRECTION

GOD WILL DIRECT YOUR LIFE

God loves you! All your life, he will hold your hand and direct you with his wisdom and counsel. He will guide you along the best pathway for your life. He will instruct you and keep watching your progress. *Psalm 32:7-8 / 73:23-24*

Footprint Just before Joshua died he gathered the people of Israel and reminded them of all God had done for them. He asked them to decide if they would serve the Lord or other gods. The people wisely chose God. Then Joshua took a large stone and placed it under a tree. It was a reminder for the people that they had promised to follow God's will. Get your own stone to remind you of your decision to follow God. *Joshua 24*

THE HOLY SPIRIT WILL LEAD YOUR STEPS

Don't be sure of your own wisdom. In everything you do, put God first and trust the Holy Spirit to lead you. He will speak to you and tell you what God wants, then you will be able to make the good decisions when your way is uncertain. For all who are led by the Spirit are children of God.
Proverbs 2:7-9 / 3:6-8 John 10:3-5 / 16:13 Romans 8:14

Footprint   Moses was a wise man, selected by God to lead the people of Israel out of slavery in Egypt. But even Moses needed God's direction. Read about the unusual way God provided direction for his people. *Exodus 13–14 Story 35*

273

GOD'S GENTLE VOICE

If you leave God's path and start to go in the wrong direction, you will hear a Voice behind you say, "No, this way; walk here." *Isaiah 30:21*

Footprint Who is easier to hear — someone yelling or someone whispering? A lot of times the world seems to be yelling at us, telling us to do this or that. But God gently, quietly whispers to us, telling us the right things to do. Read *1 Kings 19:11-13* and *Story 103* to discover how Elijah learned to listen to God.

GOD WILL SHOW YOU CLEARLY THE WAY YOU ARE TO GO

God doesn't want you to be like a senseless mule that has to have a bit in its mouth to keep it in line. He is your friend, he will tell you clearly what you need to do next. He will light your pathway and make it smooth and straight; it will be plain to follow. *Psalm 27:11 / 32:7-9 John 15:15*

Footprint   Read how God let Balaam know that he was being like a stubborn mule that needed to be forced into obedience. *Numbers 22 Story 52*

GOD WILL BRING HIS PLAN TO PASS IN YOUR LIFE

If you're being obedient to do what the Lord shows you each day, then you will stay on the right path, and the final outcome of your life will be exactly what God had planned.
Psalm 25:8-10 Proverbs 16:1 / 20:24

Footprint Have you ever tried to put a new puzzle together without *ever* looking at the picture on the box? It's hard to do. Our own lives are like a puzzle. Sometimes we can see lots of the pieces, but we aren't able to see the whole picture. So obey God and follow him. He'll fit things together so that your life puzzle will look exactly like his picture.

GOD WILL REWARD YOU FOR FOLLOWING HIS DIRECTION

God has made a path through life for you. The path may be easy at times and difficult at others. But easy or hard, you can know that the Lord is with you all the way. He will work all the events of your life for your greatest good.

Psalm 25:8-10 / 32:7-9 Proverbs 3:6-8 Isaiah 42:16 Romans 8:28

Footprint   Jesus said, "If you insist on saving your life, you will lose it. Only those who throw away their lives for my sake will ever know what it means to really live." *Mark 8:35*

THE LORD IS MY SHEPHERD

Because the Lord is my Shepherd,
I have everything I need!

He lets me rest in the meadow grass
and leads me beside the quiet streams.

He gives me new strength.

He helps me do
what honors him the most.

Even when walking through
the dark valley of death
I will not be afraid,
for you are close beside me,
guarding, guiding all the way.

You provide delicious food for me,
in the presence of my enemies.

You have welcomed me as your guest;
blessings overflow!

Your goodness and unfailing kindness
shall be with me all of my life,
and afterwards I will live with you
forever in your home. *Psalm 23*

PART
THIRTY-THREE
GROWTH

One Step at a Time

The more God teaches you, the more he expects from you, for you are responsible for what you've been taught. God takes you one step at a time so that you can first completely learn and put into practice what you already know. *Psalm 37:23-24 Luke 12:48 John 16:12-13 Hebrews 6:1-6*

Footprint   Babies can't eat steak when they are born; they start out with easy foods like milk. They would choke on anything else. God feeds us in the same way. We begin with milk and then move on to meat. That way, we grow strong as he leads us on to being spiritual adults. *1 Peter 2:1-3*

GOD KNOWS YOU'RE GROWING

God planned your whole life before you were even born. He doesn't expect more from you than you can do. Keep trying to obey him, confess your sins, and keep on growing.

Psalm 139:1, 16 John 9:41 1 John 1:7, 9

Footprint   When you were a baby, your parents thought it was OK for you to smear food on your face and chew on toys. As you grew up, they expected more from you. It's the same with God. He only expects you to do your best. When you make a mistake, he lovingly forgives you and helps you learn.

GOD WILL HELP YOU GROW

The righteous will move onward and forward. When you have a pure heart, you will become stronger and stronger. You'll flourish like a palm tree and grow tall like a cedar. For you've been transplanted into the Lord's own garden and placed under his personal care. *Job 17:8-9 Psalm 92:12-13*

Footprint   You can be a mirror that brightly reflects the glory of the Lord. And as God works in you, you will become more and more like him. *2 Corinthians 3:18*

GOD'S GOAL

God is growing and equipping all Christians to do better work for him. He wants each one to come to a position of strength and maturity, to live in unity and become full grown in the Lord, yes, to the point of being filled full of Christ.
Ephesians 4:12-13

Footprint   Under the Lord's direction every Christian is fitted together perfectly, and each one in their own special way helps the others so that each one is healthy and growing and full of love. *Ephesians 4:15-16 Story 198*

A Right Time for Everything

A time to be born;
A time to die;
   A time to plant;
   A time to harvest;
A time to kill;
A time to heal;
   A time to destroy;
   A time to rebuild;
A time to cry;
A time to laugh;
   A time to grieve;
   A time to dance;
A time for scattering stones;
A time for gathering stones;
   A time to hug;
   A time not to hug;
A time to find;
A time to lose;
   A time for keeping;
   A time for throwing away;
A time to tear;
A time repair;
   A time to be quiet;
   A time to speak up;
A time for loving;
A time for hating;
   A time for war;
   A time for peace.

Ecclesiastes 3

PART THIRTY-FOUR

WHEN JESUS COMES AGAIN

JESUS WILL COME AGAIN

COUNT DOWN
10 9 8 7 6 5 4 3 2 1

THE
LORD'S
HORSE
REVELATION 19:11

After Jesus had risen into the sky and disappeared into a cloud, two angels told his disciples that he had gone away to heaven but would return someday! Look forward to it, for when Christ who is your real life comes back again, you will shine with him and share in all his glories.
Acts 1:9-11 Colossians 3:4

Footprint   Only God knows the date when the world will end. Only God knows. And he does not want anyone to perish. Instead he wants everyone to learn to love and trust him so that they can live beyond the end of the world with him in heaven. *Matthew 24:36 2 Peter 3:9 Story 170*

GOD IS PLANNING
A NEW HEAVEN AND EARTH

When Jesus comes again, the earth and the sky will disappear to make room for a new heaven and a new earth that God has promised. There will be only goodness on this wonderful new earth and it will be so much better than the old one that we will never miss it. *Isaiah 65:17 2 Peter 3:13*

Footprint   Once God has set up the new heaven and earth, he'll live there with you forever. *Revelation 21:1-3*

287

THE NEW JERUSALEM

When Jesus returns, you will live with God in a city like you have never seen! It will not be like cities now, with smog and dirt and noise. It will be peaceful—full of goodness and gold and jewels. We will not need the sun because God's light will be more than enough. He will be worshipped everywhere in the city and nothing evil will ever come near it. *Revelation 21:10-27 Story 206*

Footprint   This city and new life with God are waiting for you if you follow him.

288

NO MORE CRYING

When Jesus returns, all tears will be wiped away, there will be no more death nor sorrow, nor crying, nor pain. All of that will have gone forever. *Revelation 21:4*

Footprint   These things are results of sin. Before sin came into the world, Adam and Eve didn't even know what crying and sorrow were. *Genesis 1–3 Stories 1–2*

289

YOU WILL BE GIVEN A NEW BODY

When Jesus comes back he will take your body and change it into a wonderful, perfect body, full of strength and glory just like his own. It will never grow tired or die.
1 Corinthians 15:45-50 Philippians 3:21

Footprint   After Jesus rose from the dead he never got tired, and he could appear and disappear and travel back and forth from heaven to earth. He had the qualities of a man and a spirit. *Luke 24:31, 36, 39, 43, 51 John 20:17, 27 Story 178*

GOD'S CREATION AT PEACE

All creation is waiting patiently for that future day when Jesus will return. For then all the things that bring pain and suffering into the world—will disappear at God's command. All the things that God created will be free again and will share God's happiness forever. *Romans 8:19-22*

Footprint God says the wolf and lamb shall play together, and snakes won't bite anymore! *Isaiah 65:25*

WHEN WILL JESUS COME AGAIN?

"Jesus, what events will signal your return and the end of the world?" asked his disciples.

Jesus told them, "Don't let anyone fool you. For many will come claiming to be the Messiah and will lead many astray. The nations and kingdoms of the earth will rise against each other, and there will be famines and earthquakes in many places. But all this will be only the beginning.

"The Good News about the Kingdom will be preached throughout the whole world, so that all nations will hear it, and then, finally, the end will come.

"Then if anyone tells you, 'The Messiah has arrived at such and such a place or has appeared here or there,' don't believe it. For false Christs shall arise, and false prophets, and will do wonderful miracles, so that if it were possible, even God's chosen ones would be deceived. See, I have warned you.

"So if someone tells you the Messiah has returned and is out in the desert, don't bother to go and look. Or if they say that he is hiding at a certain place, don't believe! For as the lightning flashes across the sky from east to west, so shall my coming be, when I, the Messiah, return. The nations of the world will see me arrive in the clouds of heaven, with power and great glory. And I shall send forth my angels with the sound of a mighty trumpet blast, and they shall gather my chosen ones from the farthest ends of the earth and heaven.

"Heaven and earth will disappear, but my words remain forever. But no one knows the date and hour when the end will be — not even the angels. No, nor even God's son. Only the Father knows. Blessings on you if I return and find you faithfully doing your work." *Matthew 24*

PART THIRTY-FIVE
FRIENDS

THE REWARD OF FRIENDSHIP

You and a friend can accomplish twice as much as you could by yourself. Even in war, if a soldier is alone he'll be defeated, but if others fight with him, together, they have a chance. *Ecclesiastes 4:9-12*

Footprint When friends pray together about something, their prayer is much more effective, in fact, God guarantees results. Read *Matthew 18:19*. Remember the story about Jonathan and his armor-bearer? *1 Samuel 14:7 Story 78*

LOYAL FRIENDS

The kind of friend that you are is the kind you'll end up having. God says you should forget your friends' mistakes, pray for them, never speak unkindly about them or to them, and never abandon them when they need your help. Then you'll always have friends who are willing to help you.
Job 42:10 Proverbs 16:28 / 17:9, 17 / 18:24 / 27:10, 17, 19

Footprint   An unreliable friend is like a brook; it floods when there is ice and snow, but in the hot weather it disappears. Jesus is your reliable friend. He promises never to leave you. Ask him to help you be a good friend to others.
Job 6:15-18

GOD WILL HELP YOU CHOOSE THE RIGHT FRIENDS

God wants you to enjoy the companionship of those who love him and have pure hearts, for you will become like the people you spend time with. Keep living in the light of God's presence and you'll find friends there.

Proverbs 13:20 2 Corinthians 6:14-18 2 Timothy 2:22 1 John 1:7

Footprint   David and Jonathan promised to love and help each other no matter what the cost. Jesus wants you to have that kind of friendship with every one of God's children. *1 Samuel 18:1-3 1 John 1:7 Story 82*

FRIENDS AND FAMILY FOREVER

When a Christian friend or family member dies, you don't have to be full of sorrow. They've gone to heaven to be with the Lord. So you'll only be apart from them for a short time, and then you will be with them forever. They are watching you now from heaven!

2 Corinthians 5:8 1 Thessalonians 4:13-18 Hebrews 12:1

Footprint   Paul said, "For to me, living means opportunities for Christ, and dying—well, that's better yet!" *Philippians 1:21-23*

MY FRIENDS

There are many people
Whom I call my friends.
People whom I know,
I wave at them to say hello.
People whom I see,
I recognize them, and they recognize me.
Some, I don't even know their names,
But their smiles to me are their friendship claims.

There are many people
Whom I call my friends.
People whom I know,
They stop by to say hello.
People whom I see,
I talk to them, and they talk to me.
These people, I know more than their names,
And their times with me are their friendship claims.

There are many people
Whom I call my friends.
People whom I know,
We get together to say hello.
People whom I see,
I'm close to them, and they're close to me.
I know their hearts as well as their names,
And their love for me is their friendship claim.

But there's only one friend
Whom I call my best.
Him I know,
I pray to him to say hello.
Him I see,
When I read his Word, and he talks to me.
I've known him since I called his name,
For the death of his Son is my friendship claim.

PART THIRTY-SIX
THE BOOK

GOD'S WORD WILL STRENGTHEN YOU

You need physical food to strengthen your body. But more importantly, you need spiritual food to strengthen your spirit and soul. God's Word is that spiritual food, strengthening you with joy, patience and encouragement.

Job 23:11-12 Isaiah 55:2-3 Jeremiah 15:16 Romans 15:4

Footprint Trust God to feed you daily from his Word, just like he fed manna daily to the people of Israel.

Exodus 16:14-16 Story 36

GOD WILL HELP YOU UNDERSTAND THE BIBLE

When you read and study God's Word, ask him to give you the wisdom to see clearly and really understand what you're reading. Then the Holy Spirit inside you will teach you and cause you to understand the great truths of God's Word. *1 Corinthians 14:6 2 Corinthians 4:6 Ephesians 1:16-18 1 John 2:27*

Footprint   Jesus told the people a story about a farmer who planted some seed. He was talking about himself, planting God's Word in your heart. Ask God to make your heart like the good ground so that you can hear and understand his Word. *Matthew 13 Story 156*

GOD'S WORD WILL CAUSE YOU TO GROW

The whole Bible was given to us by inspiration from God and is useful to teach us what is true and to make us realize what is wrong in our lives. It straightens you out and helps you do what is right. It is God's way of making you able to do good to everyone. *2 Timothy 3:16-17*

Footprint Know what God's Word says and what it means! The Pharisees knew all about God's law, but they didn't know what it meant. They did not allow God's Word to grow in their hearts. Don't make the same mistake. *Matthew 5:20*

302

GOD'S WORD IS FULL OF POWER

God's Word is full of living power! Whenever he speaks he sends the power to get the job done with the words. So as you learn and believe God's Word, his power will go down into your deepest thoughts and desires and get his job done in your heart. *Isaiah 55:11 Hebrews 1:3 / 4:12*

Footprint And the promise of God's power is for others too. When you speak God's words about Jesus and salvation, God's power will be there to bring others to Christ. *Romans 1:16 Story 184*

GOD'S WORD IS TRUE

The whole Bible was given to you by inspiration from God. Even though all heaven and earth disappear, God's Word will remain true forever. He said it, and his Spirit will make it all come true. *Isaiah 34:16 Luke 21:33 2 Timothy 3:16*

Footprint   When you read the Bible, you don't ever have to wonder if what you are reading is true. No prophecy recorded in Scripture was ever thought up by the prophet himself. It was the Holy Spirit who gave these godly men true messages from God. *2 Peter 1:20-21 Story 127*

GOD'S WORD WILL PURIFY YOU

How can you stay pure? By reading the Bible, for God's words will wash you, making you holy and clean.
Psalm 119:9 John 15:3 / 17:17 Ephesians 5:25-27

Footprint   Through the washing of God's Word, Jesus is making his whole church glorious, without spot or wrinkle or any other blemish—holy without a single fault.
Ephesians 5:26-27

GOD WILL REWARD YOU FOR STUDYING HIS WORD

Just casually reading God's Word is like glancing at yourself quickly in a mirror, then trying to fix the way you look after walking away. You've forgotten what you saw. But if you keep looking steadily into God's Word, you will not only remember it, but you will do what it says, and God will greatly bless you.
James 1:23-25

Footprint   Read *Matthew 13:14-16,* and ask God to give you seeing eyes, listening ears, and an open heart.

306

GOD'S WORD IS A LIGHT

When you spend time reading God's Word, he will light up your mind with understanding, and you will not stumble on your path in life. *2 Peter 1:19*

Footprint David said, "Your words are a light for the path ahead of me to keep me from stumbling. I will obey these wonderful laws of yours." Make this your promise too. *Psalm 119:105*

307

DAVID'S PRAYER

How can a young person stay pure? By reading your Book and following its directions.

I have thought a lot about the things your Book says. I've stored them in my heart so that they would hold me back from sin.

I repeat your words from memory; they are more important to me than riches.

I think about them all the time, never forgetting them. Open my eyes and help me to understand the wonderful truths in your Book. I am a visitor here on earth, and I need a map. Your Book is my map, it guides me through this life; it is my light and my counselor.

I love to read your Book; it is my comfort. I will concentrate my thoughts on your words.

Help me to love everything your Book says, your every wish; then I will never be ashamed of myself. Your Book stands firm in heaven, forever. I will quietly keep my mind on its promises.

Nothing is perfect except your words. They give me wisdom and understanding. They are a flashlight to light the path ahead of me and to keep me from stumbling.

Lord, teach me to obey your words, and give me the common sense to apply them to everything I do.

Those who love your word have great peace of heart and mind and do not fall. *Psalm 119*

PROMISE FINDER INDEX

PART EIGHT
STAYING ON THE PATH

PART NINE
GOD WILL KEEP YOU

PART TEN
FORGIVENESS

PART ELEVEN
TRUTH

317

PART THIRTY-SIX

THE BOOK